Life
RELOADED

Life RELOADED

Real-Life Stories Curated by
SANJEEV KOTNALA

Penman Books

Office No. 303, Kumar House Building,
D Block, Central Market, Opp PVR Cinema,
Prashant Vihar, Delhi 110085, India

Website: www.penmanbooks.com
Email: publish@penmanbooks.com

First Published by Penman Books 2019
Copyright © Intradia World
All Rights Reserved.

Title: Life Reloaded
ISBN: 978-93-89024-17-3

Dedicated to

My father, Late Shri Ram Ballabh Kotnala.

He blesses me every moment of my life.

My mother, Smt Kanchan Lata Kotnala.

My foundation and guiding force.

My wife, Neha, my source of encouragement.

My son Prateek & daughter Preetica
for believing in me.

Every Story Finds Its Audience

Thank You Dad

I was high. I had made it to IIM Ahmedabad. For me, a new path had opened.

While I was leaving for the Institute, my father said to me, "Learning never stops."

It did not mean much to me. Maybe it should have.

Two years later, when I was about to start my career and leave for Delhi to join Eicher GoodEarth (which I never did) he said 'Sunny, your real education starts now'.

At that time, I did not relate to it.

I recall I was confused.

Was my education not over?

However, I did not seek an explanation.

I missed the point entirely.

The last time he pushed this kind of agenda was when I was discussing a part of my life with him; he paused and said 'if you are open to suggestions and willing to observe and learn, there is something for you at every stage of life. You will never find a better teacher than life'.

No, I did not get the message even then.

It all came back three decades later. I am now a Brand and Marketing advisor, an accredited coach and have created a successful program called 'BRAND-i'.

Experiences mould our attitude ad approach to life. They are the reason for our success. Our conscious and unconscious learning is like tectonic plates. We only realise their presence when earthquake hits us.

We are ultimately the result of the choices we make. In addition to a Learning attitude, we must have a Reflecting attitude. We must have the courage and willingness to reflect on every episode of our life. Synthesise learning, absorb them and move on..

That was the day; I understood what my father has been hinting at. Pause. Reflect. Absorb the learning. Drop the baggage associated with that episode in life and Move-on.

Sanjeev Kotnala

Life Reloaded
RAM: Reflect. Absorb. Move on.

Life is like a mega television serial with episodes that are continuous. Emotions, actions and reactions, creating a crisscrossed path of an unexplained journey to a destination no one wants. These episodes of life have hidden lessons you may or may not want to decipher.

In Indian culture and traditions, learning from self-experience is a central theme. Lessons in life keep coming thick and fast, every moment of the day. It is not necessary that you learn only from your experiences. You can learn from the experience of other people.

So, why not share some episodes of life. Maybe when you reflect, you will see a differential picture, new learning.

These are not larger than life eureka moments. These are moments where one can easily miss the hidden lessons unless they reflect deep.

I thank each one of my fellow contributors for sharing a spectrum of life episodes from professional and personal life. I hope the effort will be appreciated.

Some contributors have shared their learning from the episode. It is possible that you may read between the lines and interpret them differently. After all, we all have filters, which distort, delete and generalise before we allow any message to impact us. And well, each of us has different filters in our attempt to find the patterns we want to read in a situation.

Other than the contributing authors, many others have willingly and at times unintentionally contributed to this compilation. The students and participants of 'Brand-I' sessions and workshops shared many learning incidents from their lives. It was this honest sharing of life-episodes that gave birth to the idea of this book.

With the 'Timeline' process in NLP and the resultant introspection, I realised the power of learning from self-experiences. How much I have lost by not listening to the chapters of my life.

It is tough to list all the contributors. To ensure I do not miss out anyone, I have decided to keep him or her faceless. Over tea, coffee and drinks, I have time-and-again immersed with my friends in recounting segments of life. We have discussed and dissected incidents after incidents. Each time, new nuances emerge. A different point of view gives then a new hue. Good, Bad and Ugly is just a contextual interpretation.

There are many impressions in the University of life if you would care to stop, listen and understand. Just pause a little bit, reflect unbiasedly on the life-episode, absorb the learning and move on. The story of life till now cannot be changed. However, you do have a choice to make what the next and follow-up chapters are going to be. That's how you become a better professional, a better family person- a better human being. RAM- Reflect Absorb Move on- is the mantra I share.

After reading the book, if you find, you have a life-episode you will want to share. An experience others can benefit from. Do send me your story in not more than 2500 words (Minimum 1200 words), and maybe it will be featured in the next book in this series or a blog that speaks of it. Send it at netkot@yahoo.com and in the subject line, please write RAM BOOK-II.

Contents

Nighty Bar

Khyati

Life in an advertising agency demands a lot of commitments, especially when you are just 2-3 years old in the industry. How else can you explain the 16-18 hours that I have spent with my art or copy partner or my servicing colleagues? Arguments, beer lunches, blows, after hour parties, love affairs and politics, all co-exist. Often these relationships offer the much-needed security on the way home, especially over long, late nights. Moreover, the gap between the salary and lifestyle is huge. Sometimes a colleague shares the load; usually, nobody does.

One such month replete with 'overnighters,' I was financially broke before the month began.

I needed to save desperately. I decided to travel by train since taking an auto was criminal.

The moment I took the decision; I became a nervous wreck.

The road to the station was completely deserted.

The concrete structures looked so delicate and beautiful. Moreover, the lane had rickshaws parked on both the sides in a perfect line. Almost as if someone artistic had been at work - measuring the distance from the boundary wall, before meticulously parking them aligned to each other.

I was trying my best not to get carried away with the beauty of the night.

I am a woman. I need to be aware, alert and focus on my travel back home, especially at 1.30 AM. However, this wasn't a calm kind of awareness.

It was like an alarm call, my emotions pumping in grey thoughts.

So, I did a self-check.

I was wearing a cotton salwar kameez[1] with a dupatta[2] (most important) - No provocative dressing – check! No

---

[1] A traditional Indian dress; a long tunic type upper garment with a loose baggy trouser type of lower garment.
[2] A piece of rectangular long cloth worn with a Salwar Kameez; it is draped around the neck with the ends thrown towards the back from shoulders.

valuables on – check! No make-up on me, it all disappeared in the last 16 hours. Hair tied – check! Nerdy look – check! I immediately took out my glasses and wore them. The ultimate, repulsive nerd look – Double Check!

As I made my way to the railway platform, I was shocked to see the gender disparity at its best. I could not see a single woman at the station. I heard that in most late evening trains between Dadar and Vasi, one could spot the women vegetable vendors.

Late evening! It was 'late night'!

As I began walking to the station, I felt the deafening silence of the night.

I looked around. The partially lit station had many threatening dark corners. People were sleeping on the benches. Canteens were still wrapping up; there were streams of water running from the shops where they were washing utensils. I was watching my step, carefully trying to glide in a way that no one should notice me. In the same breath, I was also protecting myself from all the panic situations that I had begun to imagine. I imagined every look that came my way to be that of a potential rapist or murderer or a serial killer. I could hear train sirens in the distance, but there were no trains on the tracks.

Suddenly, a shadow sneaked up my shoulder. My heart started pounding in my mouth. 'Oh damn! What if he has a plan, and what if he harms me!' I began wondering if something untoward happens, will someone come forward to rescue me? Will I be left alone to die? I was so terrified and lost in my thoughts that I did not realise when the shadow disappeared. Sigh!

There was severe confusion between the 9 and 12 coach trains. I was not sure where the 24-hour ladies' compartment would halt. So I walked up to the spot where I assumed the coach would stop. However, I was not sure.

I took a wide glance at the whole station. My eyes zeroed on to one spot where a woman was seated. She was sitting cross-legged on the bench. The area was not well lit. I could feel she was wearing a cotton salwar kameez. She had a sweet oval face with sharp features. Her long hair tied into a ponytail, and there was an over-sized bag on her lap. It looked as if she had just refreshed her makeup.

As I opened my mouth to ask her about the location of the 24-hour ladies' compartment, she nodded her head in anticipation, warm and reciprocating. So much calmness at this hour, on a deserted railway station, was uncanny. It freaked me out. I reluctantly cleared my doubt. I was upset with myself to have got into a situation where I had no option but to be seen and to talk with a girl 'like her'.

I tried to look everywhere else but in her direction. I stood as far as possible from her, close enough to watch her from the corner of my eyes or hear her speak.

Her phone rang, and she quickly responded 'Kahan hai tu, mein kab se baithi hoon, tere intezaar mein'. (Where are you, I am waiting for you since long). My ears suddenly became tingled with interest not wanting to miss a word.

She further added 'Wohi aapni roz ki jagah pe baithi hoon' (I am at my regular place). Oh, my! What I am doubting is true. This girl is waiting for her client, and this must be their pick up spot. Damn! Why didn't I save some money rather than shopping the other day? I don't need the scrub I picked up… I have not even used it in the last 20 days. The seemingly smarter cells of my mind started chattering and fighting within their dumb shopaholic cells. The thoughts were interrupted by the siren of the approaching train.

As the train halted, I began to board the train, still keeping an eye on that girl. Another girl joined her, and they boarded the train right after me. For the first time in my life, the entire train was empty, and I had the opportunity to choose. I could sit wherever I wanted. I picked up the window at a safe centre row. Damn! The girls followed me and sat right next to me! The entire train was empty, and each one of us could have taken our preferred window seat. Why were they then hanging out with me? Did I at any time show interest or acknowledge their presence?

Every strand of hair on my body felt miserable with my proximity to them. As soon as they settled next to me, the first lady introduced me to her friend. She said they took this train every day. I corrected them in my head 'You mean, every night!'

Ok, I told myself, I was captive for how-many-ever minutes the train takes to reach Borivali… I had to put up with this. I promised myself, next month I will save enough money to be able to afford an auto ride throughout the month, even at the end of the month.

After having exchanged pleasant smiles with me, they continued their conversation. I was least interested; however, I could hear it in parts. They were discussing some Pantry issues and some workplace affairs. In between their conversation, the first lady asked me "why" I was travelling home so late. 'Hold on! Are you eligible to ask me that question?'

'I work for an ad agency' I snapped back. 'We have erratic schedules, and I usually take a cab, but today I decided to take a train.' I had no reason to give such a long answer. Maybe I wanted to differentiate between them and myself. I forced myself to ask her where was she working, and she replied, 'Nighty'.

No lingerie shop is open until 1.30 am in the night, and hence I was sure it was the name of a bar, … Nighty bar! They were bar girls! I was right.

As she continued her conversation, she spoke of the long work hours and the need to be paid on an hourly basis for achieving the targets. I was surprised 'What! Bar girls also have targets…what would their KRA be? How many men throw money at them or in what denomination! They spoke about American clients, and I thought to myself, ''This sounds like some advanced kind of bar where they have foreign clients as well.'

The conversation moved on to audits and taxation.

I was shocked... A bar that is sincere about taxation and audits - Wow!!

And suddenly, I heard one of them saying – laptop -- HTML coding and java process!

I quickly turned to them in utter disbelief and asked them once again –Where do you work?

This time, loud enough to cut through the noise of my mind, and she replied with equal grace and élan "IT." (Information Technology, duh!).

No One Is Above A Meal

Farzana Suri

My first advertising agency, DaCunha Advertising, seemed like *manna* from heaven. It was barely a week since I began work, there. Strangely, even at that time, I knew that the Universe treated me in a special way. From harbouring dreams of being an ad person while I was auditing as a Chartered Accountant intern, I had hit the jackpot, indeed! I was delighted to be breathing the same air as creative geniuses like Sylvester DaCunha and Bharat Dabholkar. As an Account Executive in the agency, I was assigned to the Parle Agro brand team handling Frooti and Appy. Both trend-setting beverage brands and that was a double whammy for me! It was a window of sunshine enveloping my world that was now far removed from the ecosphere of boring balance sheets and disgruntled entrepreneurs.

Everything began just as I had imagined. My first day itself was star-spangled in a glamorous company. What with the ravishing model, Rachel Reuben; the blue-eyed, child-model and poster boy, Jugal Hansraj and Arshad Warsi, the dancing sensation at that time, sashaying in to meet Bharat. As luck had ordained, I had the box seat! My cubicle was right next to the entrance. Did I love this job! And, I knew at that moment that this was my calling... I belonged here.

Having never worked beyond 6 pm in my life or beyond a 2-kilometre radius from home (we, South Bombayites are snobs, that way), I had yet to experience the 'enthralling drama' of the late nights in the ad world. The energy of the people at work was as inspiring as it was fascinating.

I witnessed, Alaka Bhosle, the Account Director preparing to leave for her gym routine at 5.30 pm in a sexy, pink coordinated tracksuit and shoes to match. My thought blurb read, 'That's how I'd like to be a few years from now!' Kunal Vijayakar, the Creative Supervisor in his ripped jeans (what we, now call an engineered pair of jeans) and Bharat with his plain-speak and quirky sense of humour preparing for the 'creative' huddle with 'The God of DaCunha', Sylvester DaCunha or Sylvie.

Each one in the agency was a role model worth emulating.

Sylvie presided over the 3Ms – Monday Morning Meetings and even a casual glance from him above his tortoise-shell framed glasses, and bushy eyebrows gave me the elated feeling that I existed in the agency! Advertising was growing on me, and I liked everything about this world!

Then, there was Maria Gomes, my immediate boss. She was one hell of a woman. In her pencil heels and over-sized bags that contained every conceivable thing she ever needed, change of shoes, notepads, pens and an assortment of women's things. Believe me; she could run faster than most women would walk with her large, heavy bag, slim heels and all. She was a woman who was always in a hurry, which resonated with the kind of work advertising demanded - then and now. Maria was slim with a bundle of energy that belied her frame and a hardball, obsessed with work. To her credit, she was damn good at what she did as well.

It was one muggy, August afternoon when the agency was buzzing more than usual. Every department was involved in the launch of a new summer campaign on Frooti. My colleague and friend, Melwyn called me over to join him for lunch in his cubicle. I had barely unwrapped my lunch and stuffed a bite in my mouth when I heard a voice screaming my name aloud. 'Farzana! FARZANA! Where are you?'

I sputtered through the mouthful, 'I'm having lunch. Could you give me 10 minutes?' 'No!' was the sharp response. Not wanting to escalate the matter, (I was a mere Account Executive after all) I hurriedly stood up and rushed out, throwing the bite of food I had almost devoured, back onto the plate.

Hands folded across her chest, feet apart, standing like one of the Justice League characters was my boss, Maria. Her piercing eyes made me speed up, and I could sense from the tone of her body. She wasn't quite happy with my response.

'This fax has to be sent, now!' she stated, in one of the most familiar statements in advertising and marketing. 'Do you realise, we will lose Parle, if this isn't sent out, right now?' I was trembling by now, and my anxious heart raced faster. She continued, 'And what's the hurry to eat? There won't be food if there is no account!'

By this time, I was numb - for many reasons. One, I had never been shouted at. Two, I thought I'd lose my job because I had my priorities wrong – career is of more important than food. Lastly, I was embarrassed because all eyes were on me!

I grabbed the letter from her hand and sprinted toward the fax machine. As I was loading it with unsteady hands, a 'theatrical', male voice boomed, 'Get back!'

I turned, consternation writ large on my face, and froze as I saw Bharat Dabholkar standing a short distance away. He repeated, quietly, 'Go back and have your lunch.'

I looked at Maria, seeking approval and glanced once again at Bharat. He was firm. His eyes, otherwise benign, seemed to have taken on a steely shade. He had his hands casually placed on the cubicle wall, his biceps taut and his face calm and composed. Maria turned to look at Bharat, not happy with this interjection. The silence that ensued after Bharat spoke, sliced through the agency buzz.

His eyes were on me. Mine were on Maria's, and the whole agency watched all of us – eyes moving from left to right and right to left. It was surreal, like watching a Grand Slam title between Bjorn Borg and Martina Navratilova. My eyes pleaded with Bharat, silently for having been placed in this uncomfortable spot. What am I supposed to do? Bharat was second-in-command, and there was no way his instruction could be ignored. I knew that.

One week old and already caught in a crossfire between the Big Boss and the Reporting Boss. Bharat continued, 'Parle can wait. Your lunch shouldn't. Go, finish your lunch' Bharat's tone and eyes were firm, 'If Parle is more interested in the fax and not your lunch, then DaCunha does not need that kind of an account. Remember,' he turned to look at the audience of this unrehearsed drama, 'no client or superior is above your food. You all work to place two square meals on the table. And, if someone or anyone does not respect that, then what the hell are you all really, working for!'

I was in a daze as I walked back to Mel's cubicle. I was bewildered and bemused. As I continued with my lunch, I had zillion emotions running through me. Respect and admiration were, perhaps the highest for the man who made me realise the value of standing up for what is important. Sometimes, it seems like staying silent is the wiser choice due to fear, and we all fall prey to it. For me, it was the embarrassment and fear of losing a job. For Maria, it was the fear of losing a client. However, Bharat placed it all in perspective.

In just 5 minutes, I had acquired more insight that afternoon than I have ever had working on the best brand campaigns in advertising.

That incident left an indelible mark on my career and my life. No matter how critical a meeting is and who I am sitting with, I ensure lunch is always taken care of. When I'm in a meeting that passes through lunch, I demand lunch. Or I schedule meeting's post or pre-lunch. The teams I've worked with across the agencies since that extraordinary day - Imageads, RK Swamy/BBDO, Lintas, Euro and Network - knew that they would never be hungry when I'm involved in the meeting.

As a Coach, I frequently narrate this ineradicable incident to my clients, often as a reminder that no one is above a meal. Not you, nor your superior, not work and nor your best client. It's beyond me, how people 'forget' to have lunch. I am equally appalled at people who conduct marathon meetings without 'remembering' to offer lunch. That's not the world I propagate, promulgate or subscribe to. Now or ever.

Thank you, Bharat Dabholkar for this prized and unforgettable life tip.

Coward

Sanjeev Kotnala

Mumbai, Late 2006. One of the leading niche channels is launching a new program. It is in JW Marriott, Juhu. It is, heavy traffic usual on the road leading to Juhu. As we get down by the gate to save those precious minutes, we are sure we are late. We avoid the customary bio break that everyone takes in Mumbai after reaching the destination. More importantly we even let go the first smoke of the evening.

It is the biggest hall in the hotel. In the corner is an enormous golden pyramid. This image will never leave my mind. I am not sure what is the relationship between the program and pyramids. Anyway, it is not relevant to the story.

Right in the middle of the hall, is the centre of our attraction, the bar. A quick glance at the counter confirms that the organisers are serving premium drinks. It is an excellent event to attend on the weekend.

Other than the colleagues I came with, I recognise many more at the party. It is going to be an exciting evening.

After a short audio-visual presentation and few speeches, the main event started. I mean the bar is open. Invitees in slow motion float towards their ultimate destination. They seamlessly align their carefully orchestrated moves with the groups they belong. Such occasions for many, is a mini-reunion at someone else's cost. Smoking and drinking is an integral part of the rituals. It is an amazing act to witness. Uncharted, unsolicited, unguided, slowly by itself, people find their way to the designated smoking area.

This is the time, when one could smoke inside the banquet hall. No designated smoking area is required; still, people prefer to get out in the open just outside the pre-function area to have the occasional smoke. It allows one to open up, talk freely. It is a safe zone for the juniors to smoke and more importantly bitch about their seniors without much fear.

Harmless nods of the head and the friends understand what is being said. Slowly, our group leaves the hall. Few of us carry our glasses.

Here is a small trivia. It takes around eight to ten minutes for a lazy smoke to finish. I finish my first smoke and realise my glass is empty. I start my slow walk towards the refilling station, the bar. It is my first of many refills that night.

As I am moving toward the centre of the hall in pursuit of a fresh drink, I see a beautiful lady going towards the unofficial smoking zone. I see her eyes lighting up as she passes me.

For a moment, I think I know her. The very next moment I am not sure.

I tap my friend on shoulder. A quick tilt of my head. He understands my question. An understanding wink and we turn for another smoke. The drink can wait.

Smoking this time is just an excuse. We want to catch a glimpse of her. Or to be truthful, we wish she catches a glimpse of us. Saying she is a stunning beauty is an understatement. She somehow does not look like the advertising media tyoes.

She is right there at the open area. We take strategic positions diagonally opposite her in the narrow balcony type of space. Now, we are blatantly admiring her.

Correction, we are honestly ogling at her. It sounds down market, and so politically incorrect, but it is what it is.

She is wearing a red sari. The sleeveless blouse has a decently deep cut. There are few sparkling bangles on her wrist. She is carrying a small silver clutch. My trained eye are able to catch all and a bit more, in that innocent first glance.

The perfume she is wearing seems familiar. I am not sure, why I feel so. Anyway, I did not remember the name of the scent, and again it is not important to the story.

I notice the manicured slim artistic fingers picking the handcrafted silver cigarette case. She opens it with a sharp tap of freshly painted nails. The colour is crimson red.

She seems to be searching for a light. It is apparent she is not carrying one or she is doing it on purpose.

My friend, a non-smoker, obliges her with my lighter. In the flicker of the flame, I see the complete face. I see that even while she is lighting the cigarette, her eyes are fixed on me. She smiles. This time there is no confusion, she is smiling for me. The eyes says it loud and clear; we have met before.

She takes the first drag. It is long and purposeful. She is holding it for me to see her. It is dramatic. It seems the drag means a lot to her. Something is playing on her mind. With the another longmpurposeful pull, she smiles again.

I do not see an opportunity or the need to start a conversation. But, my friend and I are now lost. We have no idea how to start a conversation. It is becoming embarrassing. We are just standing there and staring at her. I sheepishly start on my walk back to the bar. This time I am committed to fill my glass.

I look back. I fear she will not be there when I return.

However, to my surprise, the lovely eyes are focused on me. I am not sure why I feel she has a question for me. You don't forget faces like her. Reluctantly, I turn and continue on my pursuit of the next drink.

After some time, she is back in the hall. I felt she is there on purpose. She is tall, gorgeous and graceful. The low-cut blouse leaves very little to imagination. I can see, why almost every pair of eyes are glued on to her. She has that magantic effect on males.

I move and strategically position myself in the group. Now, I lean against the wall and can scan the wide open hall. She is right in front of me, in my line of vision. She is smiling. She is in a conversation with a group of reasonably senior industry members. I see her looking at me from the corner of her eyes.

Why would she do that?

The face is now in focus.

The name is still lost in memories.

It is getting late.

The crowd is thinning out.

I still am okay for a few more rounds of drink. I move for the refill and find her standing a few steps before the drinks counter. I find my space at the counter. Whisky with three ice cubes topped with soda. As I start walking out, I hear her say 'smoke'.

I am confused. I look around. I heard her right. More importantly, I want to be sure that the beautiful lady is addressing me? There is no doubt, the face and the smile along with the twinkle in her eyes says it all.

Suddenly, I realise, the eyes I am looking at are one of the most beautiful but sad eyes I have ever seen. They are bland, lifeless yet hypnotic. I lead her to the smoking zone.

There is no one else in the zone. We are all alone.

She tells me she is with Vikas (identity changed), a senior industry member. For a moment, I think she is his wife. I don't like the thought or the assumption. I promptly start looking for some clue that will negate it.

I know. I know that face. I am still trying to shuffle through my unwilling memory when she fires the next bouncer. She confesses she is an Escort. She tells me, Vikas is nothing but a well-paying regular client of her. She is staying in the same hotel.

I was sure she is drunk. Why will someone say something like this to a n stranger? What is her purpose? Why is she sharing all this with me?

I look at her, and I know she wasn't high. Was it the water for Vodka trick?

Bang, the name flashes. There is no doubt. Collages of images dance through my mind. I distinctly remember her. She is not sharing things randomly. She is toying with me. She is giving me clues. She wants me to remember her naturally.

She smiles as if she was reading me. 'I will not be here if the dance bars were still open. At the bars I just danced. Most of us were not in the trade. Once the bars closed, I moved to Bangalore and then Kolkata. And here I am back. I have no option but to do this'.

More than the drink, it was she who was making me weak.

She asked me, 'Don't you think, they should have never closed the dance bars?

I have no answer.

I remember having the same discussion many years ago with then a much more bubbly and enchanting Tanya.

She realises we are on the same page. She turns, and this time she deliberately takes a long drag. She smiles as she loweres her head as if she wanted to share a secret. She whisperes 'Room 1115 booked for the night by Vikas; join me for some drinks. It will be good to talk to you. Vikas will anyway take long. He is so dead anyway'.

A part of me wants to join her. A part of me wants to know her again. Know the complete story. The chapters that were written post the closure of dancing bars in

Mumbai. A part of me sincerely wants to know, and another part of me is busy imagining things.

I want to get out. I have got the last message loud and clear. The thoughtful invite is disturbing.

I leave her and walk to join the group at the bar. Vikas is tipsy but in control. The glass in his hand has been refilled recently. He is in high spirits and is looking forward to a good time.

I see Tanya too has joined the group, and she is standing right behind Vikas. I can see the keys dangling from her finger. '1115' is visible on the key. Maybe she is showing the proof and reiterating that the invition was not really casual.

It is more than a coincidence. In her eyes, I can see a purpose. I am definitely on a shaky wicket. There is nothing to doubt. She whispers something to Vikas, smile in my direction, and with the simple nod of her head leaves the hall.

Something holds me back. I stay back. Vikas has few pegs more before he calls it a night. I feel better. There is no question of Vikas being naughty tonight, he is stoned dead. The only thing he can possibly do us hit the pillow.

It is time for me to leave the hotel.

I am climbing the spiral stairs to the lobby when my mobile vibrates.

The SMS reads. 'I knew you will not come. Once a ditcher, always a ditcher. Coward. Bye.'

I close the SMS and dial a number from memory.

With complete control of self, I command 'Driver, bring the car'.

Even today, when I see Vikas, I see her.

I want to talk to her, to explain and to be guilt free.

I am sad. I am guilty.

I am a coward in many ways than I will ever accept.

The Clock Struck Zero

Lata Subramanian

My eye travelled to the clock on the bed stand and watched as the small hand worked its way laboriously to the Roman numeral I.

A sigh arose in my mind, only to be ruthlessly squashed and imprisoned. In no way could I afford to let that sigh escape and signal the wrong message to the person sitting by my bedside.

To aid my effort, I shifted my prone position ever so slightly to distract my brain and give my cramped body and mind a little wiggle room. The hand tightly clutching one of mine did not make even that movement easy.

You would think that, by now, I would have gotten used to what had grown into a nightly ritual. But I hadn't. The state of affairs was simply too discomfiting, forever shifting the balance in the parent-child relationship.

It had all begun some three weeks prior when my mother, a severe diabetic, was diagnosed with a kidney condition. The doctor we had then consulted had informed us that she would be on dialysis in around a year's time. With his pronouncement, our lives had tilted on their respective axes, spinning us out of our individual orbits.

The mother star had begun to disintegrate.

I guess it was my mother's need to preserve her life, which led to her unburdening herself to me each night. For her, it was a cleansing of the record she wished to leave behind. I understood that. But the cleansing ritual left me with a burden of knowledge that I didn't want to bear. The unvarnished truth does that to a soul. It troubles as much as it liberates.

I can't share here all the minutiae of what my mother told me all those nights ago. That would be a horrific betrayal of her confidences. But, what I can tell you is that listening to my mother share what troubled her about her life forever changed my perception of the parental figure and the process of ageing.

Till I was forced to vicariously live through the ageing process, I had always vaguely thought that old age was tantamount to the golden years of a person's life. I guess the images I bore in my pea-sized brain had been planted there by all the grandfather roles played by Ashok Kumar[1] in Hindi movies. Aficionados of Bollywood fare will know what I am talking about. The much beloved, elder patriarch of the family horsing around with the grandchildren while still guiding the family fortunes with a firm but gentle hand.

I guess I wasn't entirely to blame for assuming that my mother would be akin to Dadamoni[2] in her twilight years. She had always been the rock of her birth family and the one she created leant on her; a role her personality revelled in.

Born in 1936 or 1937, she was the second daughter in a line of 5. As a young girl, I guess she witnessed the father she adored wear himself out bringing up five daughters in a male chauvinist society. I am inferring this because she talked a lot about her father night after night, describing amongst other things how he worked two jobs. My maternal grandfather, she told me, worked 9 to 5 for

---

[1]Ashok Kumar (1911-2001) was an Indian actor who attained iconic status first as a hero and later for his character roles. Fondly called Dadamoni (meaning elder brother), Ashok Kumar often played the elder patriarch in the Hindi movies of the 1970s to 1990s.

[2]*Dadamoni* means elder brother in the Bengali language in India. The word could also be interpreted as elder statesman in a manner of speaking.

Caltex[3], an American oil firm operating in India, and then went on to toiling till 8 or 9 in the night for a small company run by a Gujarati[4] businessman.

Someone had to support the only male in the family, and my mother took on that role. She became the son of the family. Before the feminists and their ilk howl in protest at my use of the descriptive 'son', I ask that they remember that I am narrating the life of a middle-class family in pre-Independent India. Indeed, it is precisely in that background that one has to marvel at the stories I heard from Amma[5], describing her antics as a young girl.

Here's one such tale to give you an idea of why I say that my mother was the proverbial rock that guarded her family's fort.

Picture a thin, scrawny girl of around 8 years of age. Dressed in an ill-fitting frock falling well below her knees, she is standing in a mile-long queue to collect the family's monthly ration of kerosene from a government authorised dealer. Picture that same scrawny little thing scurrying home to deliver a tin can of kerosene to her mother. Cut to a scene around 30 minutes later. The little girl has now changed the way her hair is parted and dressed and is wearing another ill-fitting dress. Once again, she is waiting

---

[3]Caltex left India when the government nationalized oil firms in the mid-1970s.

[4]*Gujarati* is the name for the community hailing from the Indian state of Gujarat.

[5]*Amma* is a word for mother in several Indian languages.

in the mile-long queue outside the ration shop. When her turn comes, the harried dealer pours more kerosene into the tin can she holds out without looking too closely at either the girl or the ration card she holds out. With her can full, the girl rushes home with more kerosene to fuel the household cooking.

That was my Amma. I am told children grew up faster those days as they were expected to pitch in and help in family farm plots and household chores. Even so, I can't but marvel each time that I think about Amma pulling off her kerosene heist of a sort. Where did she get the courage? I guess it was due to the family necessity and no one else to help everywhere she looked. Someone had to step in and fill the breach.

And fill the breach she did pretty much right through her life, wading into situations to the point of sometimes, interference. Not surprisingly then, the entire family saw her as a strong, indomitable personality. I know her two daughters certainly did. Amma was the rock our foundation firmly rested on.

The knowledge that my foundation was now shaky had shattered my world. The doctor's prognosis besides, the nightly confidences felt like an 8+ earthquake on the Richter scale. No longer could I see Amma as a parental figure. She sat next to me, clutching my hand, like a vulnerable, insecure child seeking comfort from a parent.

What made the situation even more heartrending was that there was nothing I could say or do. All I could offer was a listening ear, a warm hand and the comfort of sympathetic silence.

Night after night, Mother and daughter together faced the fact that the clock of life was ticking towards the count of zero.

As it turned out, the doctor we had first consulted was way off the mark in his dastardly prognosis. Amma lived for almost seven years from that date and, her kidney condition never went even close to the possibility of dialysis.

Many other implausible events happened, though, to rock our world even more. A few months after we learnt she had a kidney condition, we discovered to our horror that she also had breast cancer.

Who knows, maybe all those nightly soul-cleansing sessions helped to prepare us to face the impending blows. They must have because my mother suffered through a lumpectomy, mastectomy and later radiation entailed by bone metastasis with incredible courage and dignity. As substantiation, I offer the fact that several of her doctors held her up as a role model for patients.

The story at home behind closed doors was somewhat different though. There, the mask of bravado often slipped to reveal a frightened soul. But even there, Amma would sometimes wait for hours till she was alone with me. You see, she didn't want to scare her grandchildren or trouble people with the burden of her ailing body or frightened state of mind.

Even with me, she tried hard to spare me worry and strain. I remember standing mute outside the bathroom door on several occasions hearing her sob inside. Sometimes, I'd awake in the wee hours of the morning to see her sitting up in her bed; her face screwed up in pain. As long as she could, she would avoid waking me and would do so only when the pain was beyond bearing. Or, when she knew she was just too shaky to waddle to the kitchen and make herself a cup of comforting coffee.

Yes, at times, Amma was still very much the parent. But there were many others when what I saw was a person who was all-too-human, made frail by a lifetime of troubling memories. On such occasions, she revealed the vulnerable person underneath it all; one who was trying to prepare for meeting her Maker.

Through all the ups and downs, we sometimes went through periods of deceptive health normalcy to give us respite. When that happened, Amma would revert to type to show the world that her body may be ailing, but her spirit was intact. That's when I would marvel at the fact that inside an ageing body resided an eternally young and immortal soul.

During those last few years with Amma, I also came to experience firsthand the importance of dignity to ageing people.

It was a realisation I took some time to come to grips with because my instinct was to treat Amma like an infant. I would rush to the kitchen to prevent her from cooking. I couldn't really be blamed because her hands were often shaky and she had already burnt herself a couple of times. But my mother didn't see it that way, and we had quite a few altercations on the matter.

Then one day, I saw the delight on her face when I ate something she had made with relish. It was at that moment that wisdom dawned. Amma needed to feel a sense of self-worth. She needed to feel she was still contributing something of value to my life. Above all, my mother needed to retain at least a semblance of her independence and dignity.

When that light bulb finally flashed over my dim head, I began giving my mother the breathing room she needed to live life to the fullest she could. It was a scary proposition, but it had to be done.

You can't wrap a human body or soul in cotton wool to preserve it. That's what I learnt as I watched my mother's body clock wind down to zero.

Today, as I look back, I count my blessings that I came to the realisation sooner rather than later. Because what it did was to free mother, daughters, grandkids etc. allowing them to have some great times in between bouts of illness.

Amma's spirit finally gave in to the torn down machinery of her body on April 21, 2009. Thankfully, we were spared from the agony of watching spreading cancer win the battle. Maybe her spirit dominated even there. Because what happened was that she developed bradycardia.

Her heart just kept slowing down till one day her pulse struck zero.

What Do You See?

Raman Kalia

American author, Brian Herbert, once said that the capacity to learn is a gift, the ability to learn is a skill, and the willingness to learn is a choice.

The choice to learn sounds nice in principle. However, in reality, it is tough to exercise and practice. Simply because making this choice means that you are acknowledging the fact that there is something missing in you.

Let me explain that.

We live in a culture that's driven towards excellence. We work in organisations where failure is frowned upon. We live in a society that fawns upon only success. And in such a world where we are always being judged, the most challenging thing to say is- I don't know.

We fear that not knowing is equivalent to stupidity. If we make a mistake, our peers will judge us. And we will be condemned to the horrors of ignominy and hells of ridicule if we cannot come up with the right answers all the time. How many of us have experienced the situation when the bosses say, 'Don't tell me your problem, tell me your solutions.'

My guess is all of us.

The education we get in schools and colleges is directed towards knowing the answers.

The culture of questions is never encouraged.

We are judged as intelligent or stupid by what we know.

The definite answers.

The final answers.

There are no marks for curiosity.

There are no prizes for asking what if or why or why not.

When we come out of our colleges and especially professional colleges, we go out with a certain arrogance about our knowledge.

We believe we are a gift to the world. Our work is now to go out and spread the light.

And I was one such young man, when I joined my first job - young, brash, Mr. know-it-all, with a haughty disdain towards everything around me. Everything I approached was with 'I know it better' or worse, 'I can do it better' mindset.

I honestly believed that I had so much to teach and nothing to learn. And obviously, there is no better place than the real world to erase such delusions of grandeur.

The company I joined was a market leader in agricultural products- pesticides, seeds, and fertilisers among other things. The name of organisations or people alluded to in this anecdote are immaterial and hence are not mentioned. Nevertheless, a look at my LinkedIn profile will solve the mystery for the curious ones.

Since I was part of the management trainee batch, we all went through our induction program. And as is with all organisations, during which we were given projects and assignments that included visiting the market. The markets in our case were rural. It meant that we had to visit the remotest of villages and interact with both retailers and farmers as part of the assignment. You know, the kind that needs the help of a true professional.

As it was with every trainee, I got my share of projects, some as part of a team and a few as an individual. The objective of the organisation from these induction programs was to familiarise the new employees with the work culture of the company and to use the time as a learning opportunity.

However, learning was not the predominant thought or even a thought, for that matter. What was running at the back of our minds, at least mine for sure was, 'Let's go there and see what is wrong and what we (I) will fix with our (my) superior intellect when we (I) get the proper role and authority.'

I would like to add here that most of the seniors in the organisations looked upon at this attitude with complete amusement. In hindsight, I am sure that they were thinking that once these greenhorns face the market, they would soon lose their illusions.

But, it is a mistake for any old-hands to have such an attitude. Every new person brings fresh eyes and as a process should be paid attention to. However, that is not the issue we are addressing here.

Coming back to my erroneous ways, even I approached each project and each travel with the same mindset. I was meeting people and interacting with them, but at no point, did I feel that they had anything to teach me.

Months passed. I did some work here, visited some factory there, and things were going on as they were supposed to. I would meet my friends over beer and regale them with my stories from the various visits and experiences and share my plans with them.

Then I got a project to research the effectiveness of our packaging for one of our products in the market. It included going to the villages and taking feedback from the retailers. In my mind, I felt that was such a futile job. Our packaging was designed by one of the best agencies. We had a research report that confirmed the packaging effectiveness on a range of parameters. With such supporting data already with us, what can a retailer tell us that would be new?

Nevertheless, what had to be done, had to be done.

I applied for my travel plans.

Just to sidestep from the narrative, the company had a rule that all trainee approvals would come from the MD's office. As a management trainee, you do not interact much with the MD. Except for the day one interaction, it was justified to think that the MD would not remember the trainees after the first meeting; a reality of our loaded pyramid hierarchies. This perception was especially acute in our case as we were a batch of twenty trainees.

It so happened that my approval did not come on time. Since I had to travel the next day, I went to the MD's office with a request for my travel approval. Back in those days, there was nothing called an open-door policy. One had to approach the secretary, and he or she would invariably ask you to wait, which could range from a few minutes to a couple of hours and then finally let you know the status. However, when I went to meet the secretary, the MD was there with her (no salacious imagination please, he was there for work). And to my shock, he addressed me by name. I was amazed that he knew my name.

I was not ready for the second shocker. Not only did he know my name. He was also aware of all the projects that I had done over the last six months. Not just mine, but he also knew of all the projects every trainee had done or was doing.

That was my first learning in the corporate world. When it comes to creating a great organisation, there is nothing that is insignificant. Great leadership is as much engaged with the micro, as they are with the macro. Employee engagement and loyalty are built around what seemingly looks like minor actions. Nevertheless, come to think of it, those are the ones that go a long way to drive motivation.

Let's get back to the story. I got my approval. The next day I was on the train, headed to Nashik. And from there, with our sales person from the region, I went to the interior villages.

I visited many shops, met many retailers, and not surprisingly, was overwhelmed by the hospitality I received (learning from that generosity, I will save it for another day). However, by and large, I was doing the exercise mechanically. Asking the obvious questions and getting platitudes back in return.

As I was going from shop to shop, I came to this particular store.

Now, let me describe that shop to you. It was the smallest shop you would ever visit. There was a counter. Behind that was the seller. There was barely enough space for two, or at the most, three customers to stand on the other side. It would be hard to breathe if a fourth person was to join in.

So I stood there and in a nonchalant manner asked the owner about his opinion about our packaging. The owner was an old man, maybe in his sixties, with the deep creases of wisdom entrenched on his face.

He looked at me and asked me in the local language if I looked behind him on the shelf and name five products that I see. So I looked at the shelf cursorily and named the five products that I saw.

After I had done the needful, the owner smiled and said that on that shelf, eighty percent of the products were from my company and the five names I had taken were of the competition. He then suggested that it should tell me all that was there to know about packaging!

Dismayed, I looked at the shelf again, giving it some more attention. I realised that he was right.

There, right in front of my eyes was the answer, and I was utterly blind to it. With his permission, I took the photograph of the shelf for the record.

That evening, I went back to the hotel, sat down and made a fresh set of questions to ask the other retailers I was to meet the next day.

Net result, the quality of work and learning improved exponentially.

Once I returned to the head office, for my presentation to the department, all I did was to put that picture up, and asked the everyone, 'What do you see?'

And surprisingly I got the same answer that I had given.

That very day, the department head called the agency and briefed them again.

I got lots of kudos, but it was not a moment of pride.

The question to ask is this- was that old man an aberration? Was he different from others? Or was he more intelligent than the others that I met before him?

The answer is an obvious no.

The mistake was entirely mine. I was closed in my thinking. It was my refusal to grow. It was my unwillingness to learn. The problem was the absence of my learning mindset.

The fact of life is that learning never stops. We can grow and improve every day. The world has much to teach. And we have a lot to learn from the world, and there is so much to discover. In his book 'Drive', Daniel Pink, writes about a concept called mastery. He writes about human motivation coming from that drive to constantly become better and always striving towards that perfection.

Sebastian Coe, the two-time Olympic gold-medal winner, once said, 'Throughout my athletics career, the overall goal was always to be a better athlete than I was at that moment - whether next week, next month or next year. The improvement was the goal. The medal was simply the ultimate reward for achieving that goal'.

So, here's the question. Who can teach us? Who can help us become better? And as I learnt that day, it is not just one person but everyone.

In the passing years, I have found great ideas from all kinds of places, from a random conversation with a friend, while playing with my kids, dialogue from a movie, a line in a book, an interaction while travelling in an auto, while going in the local train. One just needs to open up the world around oneself. And that's when the learning never stops.

Never again since that day have I ever approached a problem with the attitude that I knew the answer. It has been twenty years now since that incident, but the lesson learnt that day is still fresh in my memory, and it will continue to be so.

How we work depends on how we learn.

Even at the risk of sounding repetitive, the secret to doing continuously better work is never to stop learning. All it takes to do great work and succeed in life is a Learning Mindset. And the leanings never stops. It is every day. Every moment. From everyone.

If at any point in time you get the 'now I know everything' feeling, just pause and ask yourself, 'What do I see?'

Go Ahead

Harrish M Bhatia

February 1999. At the peak of winter in Delhi. The cold wave from the upper region of the Himalayas travelling down to the planes was not good enough to cool the heated up discussion inside the large conference room at the border of Delhi and Haryana; Mathura road to be precise.

Team LG was locked in a critical discussion. There was a heated debate with suggestive remarks and counter-arguments at base level. All the talent inside the room was focusing on ways to crack the Mumbai Market. It was not a satisfying performance for the brand there. The passionate team was busy crafting, drafting, and defining new approaches and strategies.

The coffee supply lines were open, and we were all replenishing ourselves with warm coffee as an aid to help keep the body metabolic rate high. Personally, I think that was a disguise as the internal arguments and discussions were good enough to do the job without any caffeine.

It was a high-power meeting with the heads of HR, Finance, Logistics, Manufacturing, Product Heads and the Marketing Head. If that was not enough, there was the energetic and highly passionate MD, Mr K R Kim chairing the meeting. For him, chairing the meeting was not about market presence but engagement and involvement.

Mumbai was something that had refused to work as per plans. The brand invested big-time in advertising and trade-loads in the market, it had done everything possible that the best of marketing brains and books could suggest, yet, it was selling half of what Delhi was doing, in spite of being almost of the same size.

Nothing seemed to be working in Mumbai. For some odd reasons, even the traders were not upbeat and confident. They were not genuinely pushing LG.

It was not something unexpected or new. The Mumbai trade is known for playing hardball. However, I was at the cross wire, as I was responsible for the market. Everyone in the room had something to say for the unenthusiastic response from the Mumbai market. Each person, if asked, could reel out the list of things they had done to support me and my market.

I felt drained in that situation. It was tough to remain calm in that room to defend the team. The people who were not at ground zero were busy commenting on the situation. It was all perceptions with no real understanding of the situation. To me, everyone seemed to be criticising my team efforts and output. Nevertheless, I remained calm.

I was up against a wall of corporate heavyweights. The discussion derailed and started focusing on scrutinising my team's capabilities. The team inside the room was busy digging holes in my team's approach and dedication.

It was apparent to me that the Head Office was on the edge of losing patience. I could completely understand it. At the same time, I had this inherent belief that given the right inputs, my team at Mumbai was capable of turning the tide in our favour.

For it to happen, it was for me to impress upon the powers that decided on such sensitive matters. On top of that, I was relatively new to the company. You can say everyone else in that room had invested more time with the company than me. The issues of credibility and proven understanding of the market would time and again short-circuit the discussion. Unfortunately, I didn't have much experience with this new responsibility.

I was determined not to give in. I believed it was not fair to be scrutinised and spoken in this critical way without the team having been provided with the inputs; they demanded to churn the market. It was clear that pushing that envelope right now would lead to a deadlock.

It required a different approach and here is when I decided to stick my neck out.

'Kill me later if you have to but allow me to run the market for three months the way I believe we should run it. I know what I am asking for, and I know the consequences of the failure as I speak. But then there is no point in attempting to manage a market as critical as Mumbai with my hands all tied. I want to be let free, and I take on the responsibility on my shoulders completely.'

I finished speaking and could hear the loud booming pin drop silence in the room. People were shocked is an understatement.

Here was a guy under whom the territory was not performing. He had the guts to demand a free hand. He wanted to run the market his way and only his way!

I also knew that I had over-stepped the conventional lines of corporate hierarchy.

It was immaterial that my voice was echoing my fundamental beliefs. Nevertheless, it was not the classic way for a field manager to challenge and take on the people at head office.

The silence was unnerving.

Suddenly, Mr. K R Kim moved up his chair. He stayed silent watching the entire drama unfold. He, now, decided to speak up. It was typical of him to do so. He demanded that I should re-state in a single sentence what I had just said.

I could see all eyes scrutinising me. I knew somewhere there were many who wanted to see me backtracking on my voice and give in. Or maybe give up and seek a transfer.

All kinds of thoughts were a riot in my mind. Neither did I have another job offer, and nor did I want to relocate my family so soon. Will it come to this? Was I not risking everything I had? What will my wife say to relocation so soon? She and the kids were just starting to settle down in Mumbai.

I took a deep breath and gathered my composure. It was perhaps one opportunity to stick my neck out and risk it all, for it is better to fight and die on your terms than being killed doing regular stuff.

'Sir, I want to be given a free hand to manage all marketing inputs to compliment my team's efforts in the field for three months.' I said in a manner that was more conversational than a stance.

However, this time there was a virtual revolt. Everyone except Mr. Kim screamed a 'no'.

The HO team was not born yesterday. They were corporate smart. They understood what I was asking. They knew the consequence and maybe a precedent creating a moment when they saw one.

I had in one sentence asked all the marketing budgets from Head office to trust me. I had asked for a complete free-hand to decide on where and how I should allocate the resources. It was against the norm. It was immaterial to me, what they were thinking and how they would react to this change of responsibility, accountability and associated power. I was convinced that if given my wish, I will be able to manage my resources in a more efficient and effective manner in the market than it has been ever done.

After everyone had shot down the brilliant idea, Mr. Kim spoke again. He had always been a man of few words, and I knew a yes or no from him would seal my fate. He just said 'Go ahead'! And he started to walk out of the room.

Everyone in the room, including me was stunned.

He reached the door and turned around to say this: 'Harrish, you better turn it around in three months or else…' He didn't finish the sentence, but he delivered the message loud and clear.

The next three months were a blur to me. The concept of day and night merged. There was no sense of time. Every moment was about market visits, negotiations, meetings with the team, advertising agencies, and vendors. I was aware what I had put on the line. It was not just my job at LG but everything I had built. It was my reputation in sales.

Our efforts started to show results. Trade too acknowledged the efforts made by the team. There was a new-found trust replacing initial reluctance. It seemed I could do everything possible to make things work.

It took us about ten weeks to start getting visible positive results. By the sixteenth week, things were turning around. The efforts were being appreciated, and my neck was no longer under threat.

It was clear to me. I succeeded because of our knowledge of the market we were operating in. There was nothing that could replace it. And secondly, that, if I had done the homework well, I could stick my neck out and take responsibility without bowing down or getting pressurised by the hierarchies, norms and expectation.

Disable Disability

Vikas Mehta

Just before the turn of the century, I started getting some noises in my ears. It was not a distraction but was definitely an irritation. I was in my early 30s happily married, upwardly mobile. I had just got my first international posting, and the world was mine to conquer. Within months, it all came crashing down.

While in Egypt, I was diagnosed with Meniere's disease. It's not a life-threatening illness. However, it is a social taboo illness. It affects the hearing and sometimes causes vertigo. Its cause is yet unknown but is linked to an unhealthy lifestyle and anxiety at the workplace, irregular eating and sleeping habits, processed food rich in sodium, cola and caffeine culture... all of which I was guilty of. There is no cure, but one needs to take preventive measures. I went for a diagnosis and treatment to the UK and US and even got an unsuccessful surgery done in my inner ear. Nevertheless, my tinnitus in the ears kept on increasing, my hearing diminished. Frankly, more than the hearing, it was the speech discrimination which was an issue. In plain language, I could hear but was not sure of what was being spoken.

My first reaction was that this cannot be happening to me. Thankfully, my immediate second reaction was that I am going to fight it. I acquired hearing aids of the highest order to improve my speech discrimination. I changed my eating habits. I cut out all tea, coffee, colas, processed foods and salt from my food. I started daily walks and also some alternate medicine.

I never allowed it to interfere with my work. I was concentrating much harder, was more focused, I even developed a bit of lip reading! And the results showed. Some of my best years in terms of results happened in Egypt and Indonesia. In Egypt, I turned around an ailing division, restored client confidence in the agency on all globally aligned MNC clients and broke all records in client performance appraisals and bonuses. Precisely the same results came in Indonesia too where I was leading a team of more than 50 people and also handling regional responsibility, which meant extensive travel throughout Asia and London.

However, I noticed another change in the way society started dealing with me. I was no more a high flyer or a rising star. I was not shunned, but when people realised I was wearing hearing aids, suddenly there would be doubts in their eyes and actions. Since I was wearing a hearing aid, therefore, it was assumed that I was at a handicap. People would raise their voice automatically, repeat the same things twice and if I asked them to repeat what they said would look at me with pity. First, I thought it was my mind playing tricks, but on closer observation, I realised it was a definite behaviour trait.

Worse was to follow. People started assuming that I was getting dumber. I could see exasperation setting in if I did not follow something at the first attempt. I could see impatience because it was assumed that having a handicap meant that I had become an inferior person.

And then the worst social behaviour emerged. I would notice people sniggering behind my back. If I misinterpreted something, it was because I was hard of hearing, and I did face some moments when people took advantage of my condition. There were some colleagues and also superiors who blatantly lied, 'But I told you so. Oh! You may not have heard it!' There were times when I knew that someone was trying to shift blame on me and use my problem to their advantage, and I could do nothing about it. It was almost as if I was marked out.

Mind you; I was in a communication business. I was at the beck and call of my clients 24x7. Plus, I had to always keep in touch with my consumers too. Attending group discussions, strategy meetings, new business pitches were all a regular part of my day. It was a high pressure, result oriented, deadline driven career.

All this did get to me. It was not only frustrating but also dealt a severe blow to my self-confidence. Maybe, I actually didn't hear what he had said? Maybe, my mind was not processing information with the same precision? Maybe, I was not capable of handling big projects? Maybe, I should retire and look at a more sedate profession?

My strength was my wife. She not only believed in me but was my walking-talking medical advisor. She would be on the net for hours surfing for more information on the disease. She would look at all types of alternate medicines. She would become part of medical groups or patient groups related to the illness. She would restore my self-confidence, and she would urge me not to give up. She always looked at the brighter side of things. At least, it is not a life-threatening disease, would be her usual refrain. That certainly put things in perspective.

The interesting part was that while I was being set up for failure due to societal and even peer rejection, my results at the workplace weren't bad at all. Yes, there were hiccups and lows, but then these happened when my confidence was at the lowest. In fact, more often than not, I realised that my clients were very appreciative, but my industry and peers were not. The word was out on the street. He wears a hearing aid. Poor fellow, he has lost it.

I was frustrated and down in the dumps. I started withdrawing into a shell. I was never a firm believer, but I started losing faith in God and even humanity. I would decline invites to clients social meets. I would shun office group events. I would not be part of any weekend outing trips.... The more I secluded and cut myself off, the more tongues wagged. The more people became convinced that I was no more a capable professional or even a friend.

I recovered with the help of my family support system. Luckily, the worst in terms of the disease got over within a few years. My ears stabilised and I doggedly got back into my groove. My life perspective had changed, and I was now determined to change some more people's.

This is not an attempt to make a victim of myself. I don't want this piece to get me sympathy. However, I think there has to be an understanding of how some acquired physical disability does not make the person less than what he used to be. How can society and workplace change their impression of someone just because he is using a device which has him labelled, handicapped? Just because I had become poor in one of my physical faculties did not mean that I had diminished as a person.

It is funny. If I had a heart attack, and I had survived it, I would have been more accepted than as a person who has got a disability. Isn't that ironic?

So I soldiered on. Bagged new assignments, made a difference in my job. However, the fact that I wore hearing aids always caught up.

Our society is full of preconceived notions. In as much as we try, it is not easy to fight and break these opinions. My experience shows me that no one will fight for you. If you are lucky as me and have a good support system like my wife, my family, my in-laws, then you can fight. But, what about those who do not have such a support system. What do those people do? How do they challenge these pre-conceived notions? What do they do? How do they survive? What about the economics of it all?

I come from a typical middle-class family with no family trusts or land holdings to support me. I am self-made and am proud of it. The economic compulsion was definitely a motivator for me to fight on. But what about the silent majority who just wither away in the face of financial hardships?

I turned fifty 18 months ago... According to our customs and belief, this is an age when a person gets into Vanaprastha ashram. Give up worldly goods; emotionally detach yourself from the world; give up the materialistic things. I did none of that for I wanted to be a role model, for I am a survivor who has survived to tell his tale.

I want to tell everyone who has a disability that they are not inferior. They are just differently abled. I want them not to accept sympathy. I want them not to expect a warm, accommodating society. I want them not to accept preconceived notions. I want them not to disrespect their own self- belief.

I want them to understand that the only disability in life is the wrong attitude.

I want them to know that they may be disabled in one aspect, but they are better than the abled in many more dimensions as they will always try harder. I want them to understand that they can be more compassionate as they realise another's pain.

I want this compassion to drive them. I want their disability to drive them. I want the hostile world to drive them. I want the sympathetic looks to drive them. And I want the desire to prove the preconceived notions wrong to drive them.

And I need your help to help them. From today when you meet a disabled person, do not treat him as a differently abled person. Respect him for what he is. Motivate him, encourage him and look at his strengths. Help him fight any preconceived notion. If you find any other person doing the opposite of this, just tick him off. Educate your children on these issues. In fact, introduce them to differently challenged people. Let them know that they are no different than anyone else.

Ultimately, it's not about apang (disabled) or divyang (new, more politically-correct nomenclature, meaning blessed organ). It's all about the manobal (mental strength) or manovriti (attitude).

No Rushing

Raja Mitra

By the time I joined one of the largest Print Media Organizations of the country as Revenue head of one of the regions, I had spent some thirteen years in the corporate jungle. Trust me that IIMs teach you a lot, but that does not necessarily make you combat ready. The new assignment had its own vignette of challenges.

I was expected to turn around a grossly under performing advertising revenue region and build to create that desirable B2B brand through aggressive marketing. One of the challenges was to stabilise and build an otherwise vulnerable team. The team was under performing. They knew it and hence were demotivated, demoralised and disheartened. On top of that, the last twelve months had seen four changes in leadership, and I was seen as another co-passenger in transit. I had to take care of this perception too. And if all this was not enough, the Human-Resource head debriefs suggested significant indiscipline and basic hygiene issues.

What the place needed was just a strong, committed and passionate hand to address the issues and resolve all the problem areas which was easier said than done.

I was operating out of the Regional Headquarters (RHQ) at Bangalore. It controlled the other four sub divisions or branch offices in the south of India. The fluidity of structure meant that there were more than the desired number of local representatives from sub-divisions reporting to the RHQ.

Each branch office was under a Branch Manager. Even though Regional Headquarters was at Bangalore, it too had its own Branch manager. The Branch Managers reported to the Regional Head, which incidentally was yours truly.

Finally, the day came, and I walked in at the Regional Headquarter brimming with excitement and enthusiasm. I reached much before the scheduled office opening time, 1000 Hrs. I did not have to wait much, and the day started with the customary round of introductions and greetings.

Then there were those brief calls to and from my immediate senior, H.R.Head and other corporate heads.

I settled down in my workstation, which was a somewhat secluded cabin at one end of the otherwise relatively large office. I thought it must have been a deliberate move to provide the Regional head with some silence and privacy. I smiled at these thoughts crossing my mind and pushed myself to address the job areas which could help me learn fast.

It was nearly noon when I decided to take a small aimless stroll through the office. My way of 'Managing by walking the corridors'. I wanted to relax. I had been laboriously working sitting at the same place for the last 2 hours.

I reached the reception and was looking around when I noticed a young, smartly dressed and athletically built gentleman casually getting in. Holy cow, I realised this person was reporting to office two full hours late!! But he didn't demonstrate any guilt. Nor was he hurrying. He did not show even an iota of respect for the new Regional Head; otherwise at least today, this guy would have been on time.

I realised that this was time to take charge. I approached him, introduced myself and asked his name. The guy replied smiling 'Good Afternoon, Sir. I am 'Naveen' (name changed). I work as a Marketing Executive in 'Subrat's (name changed) team. I report to…….'

I was not interested in the genealogy of his reporting structure. He was like the panda (priest) at Haridwar (the place where Kumbh is held) tracing your ancestors.

My next question was obvious. 'Good afternoon Naveen, it's a pleasure meeting you, but why are you so late?'

Naveen continuing with the same casual irritating smile answered, 'Sorry Sir, I had some personal work.'

'Did you inform your immediate superior or admin team about this delay?' I asked.

Naveen continued 'Hmm... Well... actually... No, Sir. It happened suddenly.'

It was not the reply that I expected or wanted to hear. I did not want to create a scene at the reception. I told 'Naveen' to continue with his work and went back to my cabin. 'Discipline and Hygiene' were two words playing loudly in my head.

From that day, I nicknamed Naveen as 'LL' or 'Late Latif'. I was now determined to keep a tab on him. I was upset with Naveen and his lazy smiling approach. One part of me was telling me that he was quite a bright and honest professional, and on the other side, his attitude was bugging me.

I picked the intercom and shared the incident with both the administrative head and the local Branch Manager. I asked them to ensure that Mr. Naveen must not repeat the behaviour. I cautioned them that one errant was enough to violate the office discipline.

From that day, Mr. Late Latif was in my radar. I was personally keeping a tab on him. It became almost a daily routine. I would step out of my cabin at around 1200 hours and casually glance at 'LL's workstation. Most of the time I was not disappointed. In the first seven days, for a few days, I found he was yet to report to the office. Another thing that hit me was that Late Latif was prompt as far as closing time was concerned, and he left the office every day on time, on the dot.

When it became too much, I lost my cool. I called him to my cabin. Without wasting time or giving him any chance to present his case, I started shouting at him. I was at the top of my booming voice, yet the only words that Mr Late Latif (Naveen) uttered in the 15 minutes of hurricane scolding were ' Sorry Sir… Sorry Sir'. I lost count of times he said sorry. I let him go with a warning.

My job needed me to travel a lot. For the next three months, I was busy visiting many regional offices, print centres and my own branch offices in the South. When finally I found some peace from this hectic travelling and found myself at the Bangalore office, my sixth sense prompted me to check on my centre of attraction, our Mr. Late Latif.

The admin person brought me the attendance report. I was horrified to note that 'LL' was on leave for fifty-one days of the ninety days. That made it more than 50% of the working days. Moreover, if that was not enough, Late Latif was late most of the other days.

It seemed as if he was testing my limit. According to me, it called for immediate action or things could get out of control.

Without wasting any time, I sent a show cause mail to Mr. Late Latif consciously marking copies to the Corporate HR, all Corporate Heads, local Branch Manager and a few more. He was asked to explain, 'Why action should not be taken against him for this irresponsible and indiscipline way'. My note went to the extent of cautioning him, that he could lose the job if he did not mend his ways or could not give a satisfactory explanation.

I don't know what made me rethink. It was like I was too harsh. Was I acting in unnecessary haste? Did late Latif Naveen not deserve a patient hearing? I was suddenly not sure of anything.

I called the branch manager for a confidential discussion. The discussion was a real eye-opener for me.

Mr. Late Latif had joined the organisation a year back, and he came from an entirely different industry. He was a keen sportsperson and as per the impression a clear thinker. Unfortunately, from day-one, he was assigned to an underachiever. This person had no vision, knowledge or passion for learning.

Naveen's problem was becoming clear to me. He had every reason to be disappointed and demotivated with the immediate leadership quality. His disillusionment from office work pushed him towards his escape; regular sports. Moreover, coming from a different industry and being a keen learner, he was much interested in acquiring the requisite knowledge and learning the nuances. In this pursuit, his senior was of no help to him.

I wanted to dig deeper and understand it a bit more. My own learning said that a sports person could be anything but insincere or negligent. I opted for a one-on-one with him. I wanted to reassure myself.

I had some buffer in the next few days. I decided to commit myself to unravel the mystery of Late Latif.

My gut feeling was right. However, the damage was done. I had to find a way to undo it.

I wrote another mail addressing all the past recipients. Referring to my discussions with Naveen, I informed them that he had assured me of his full commitment and best efforts in the future.

Over the next three months, I, along with the Branch Manager and with due approval from top management, made few much-needed changes in the structure.

Assigning Naveen (our Mr. Late Latif) to a new and more charged up senior proved to be a masterstroke. Not only did his approach to work change polarity, but soon he became the most popular person in the whole office.

Fast-forward by two years; LL is a successful leader mentoring young professionals.

The last I heard, Late Latif has taken over my position!

He is no longer late. I have fondly renamed him TL. TRUE LEADER.

Come to think of it; I almost ruined his career.

What if I had not listened to his side of the story?

What if I had not taken the time to understand the real problem and acted in haste?

What if I had not given him the benefit of the doubt?

How A Twenty Second Commute Changed My Life

Sumit Roy

I guess the idea happened to save myself embarrassment. If I remember the month correctly, it was a morning in September 1985. While I was going through my 'To Do' list, I realised that I had a meeting with a client I liked a lot. Meeting with Anoop Hoon/Basab Bose, Asian Paints said my diary.

Just that we didn't really have anything interesting to present.

I was then Client Servicing Head at Ogilvy & Mather, Calcutta, and had been given the flat that Suresh Mullick had vacated. The flat was very convenient since it was just one floor above Ogilvy & Mather's two floors of offices at 1 Auckland Place, Calcutta. The commute time to work was all of twenty seconds.

I was up at daybreak, handwriting memos that I would leave at the desks of my colleagues, just to remind them of what needed to be done that day.

Just that the task that was staring at me was something, I knew we were not quite ready with. Something I should have initiated with a better brief: New Ideas for Asian Paints Shiromoni Purashkar.

Two years before that, Asian Paints had thrown us a challenge. They were the number one paints brand in most of India. Just that Eastern India, and especially West Bengal, still favoured the brands that had factories and head offices in what was then, still, Calcutta. These companies generated jobs, and understandably, the Bangali Bhadrolok were loyal to them: ICI, Jenson & Nicholson, British Paints. Asian Paints was the foreigner; the outsider.

Asian Paints wanted to be number one in West Bengal, too. Instead of creating the expected 'corporate campaign' (read -Bengali gentleman returning from his morning shopping with a Hilsa fish in one hand and an Asian Paints can in the other) we created an award that paid tribute to what the Calcuttan loved, Arts.

Every three months The Asian Paints Shiromoni Purashkar honoured the best work that had emerged in Eastern India in six categories: Literature, Theatre, Film, Dance, Fine Arts and Music.

Bengal had taken extremely well to the idea. The quarterly announcements were looked forward to. With the award events and ads announcing the winners, we did generate a pretty high share of mind for Asian Paints.

Now, in September 1985, we were running out of steam as almost all the celebrities in these disciplines had already been honoured.

The meeting, that day, was about what we should do next.

Knowing fully well that I had not come up with an inspiring enough brief, my sense of self-respect gave me an idea in the twenty seconds it took me to be in office.

I gathered the senior-most members of the team together: Bunny Suraiya was then Creative Director of the Ogilvy & Mather Calcutta Office, Derek O'Brien the Head of Copy and Biswajit Ganguly, the Head of Art.

'What if we gave awards to the best Pujas?' I said. 'An award for the Best Pandal, the Best Lighting and the Best Pratima (idol)'. I could see in the team's eyes that I had struck a chord.

'Who will judge?' came the question.

'Why, the winners of the Shiromoni Purashkars,' came the reply. After all, all of them were very highly respected artists in their own right.

When we checked the idea with Anshu Banerjee, Company Director and Manager of the Calcutta Office, he immediately concurred.

The plan had been hatched.

To Anoop Hoon and Basab Bose's credit, they instantly bought the idea.

I seem to remember that Biswajit had quickly put together an 'announcement ad'. I do remember that I did not have to present it. Just saying the words Asian Paints Sharad Shamman and explaining the concept was enough.

The 1985 Durga Puja was just around the corner.

Fortunately, Ogilvy & Mather, Calcutta at that time had as many as 50+ employees and not much work.

Our major client, Brooke Bond, had shifted to Bangalore, where our Bangalore colleagues were looking after their several coffee brands. Dunlop used to run a Puja Traffic advertisement, in collaboration with Calcutta Police, but this had fallen into a set pattern. We literally had to just change the date. Philips was active during the Pujas, but the work was already ready for release.

Calcutta soon started slowing down for the mandatory set of Puja holidays; just that Ogilvy & Mather, Calcutta decided not to take a holiday.

From having run the Dunlop Puja Map for years, we knew where all the Pujas were clustered. Calcutta was divided into several areas, and a team of two employees was entrusted to personally visit every Puja in the area allocated to them. Their job, that by Sashti (the sixth day after Mahalaya), they would have nominated the three Pujas in their allocated area that could have won.

Then on Saptami and Ashtami (the seventh and eighth day of the Pujas), the designated judges were taken to the shortlisted Pujas in all these areas.

By the time Ma Durga had been sent back to the Himalayas, the winners were announced.

In that first year, what surprised Calcutta was that it wasn't the Pujas that had the biggest budgets that won. A then unknown 'Adi Ballygunge' shared honours with a 'Maddox Square' and a 'Jodhpur Park'.

By the next year, the Puja Organisers had figured out that, while traditional Pujas were given due respect, Bollywood music blaring away was looked down on and 'Theme Pujas' were catching the judges' attention. Pujas where the Lighting, Pandal and Pratima were all built around a thematic, artistic interpretation or idea.

Winning the Asian Paints Sharad Shamman one year, immediately ensured footfalls the next year, and therefore ensured sponsorship funds.

Within the third year, Calcutta's Puja Pandals were bursting with creativity to win the now very respected

Asian Paints Sharad Shamman. 'Themed' Pujas had caught on. The tens of millions of pandal hoppers were all being 'pretend judges' and eagerly waiting to see whether their choices matched the esteemed Asian Paints Judges.

Word of mouth took over. The impact of this initiative was many times what any corporate advertising campaign could have given Asian Paints.

Asian Paints had won over the heart of the Bengali, and that was already showing in the market share in paints.

Well before the word 'viral' had been invented, I watched in awe as the idea took on a life of its own and spread.

What was wonderful was that Asian Paints had agreed to pay, as event management fees, the money that they would normally have spent on advertising. With that one initiative, I knew that one no longer had to find ways to make clients spend on advertising. One had to come up with ideas that the consumer wanted to spread.

The consumer was, indeed, the world's strongest medium.

This one Puja Award led to many more followers. All of them, together, transform Kolkata every Autumn (Sharad), for a week or more, into what must be India's biggest creative arts festival.

After 30 years, The Asian Paints Sharad Shamman is still the most coveted Puja Award, while there are now several hundred more, me-too, Puja awards.

I had no idea that the 20-second commute to my office would change Kolkata for good.

And I discovered a truth that's governed the rest of my career.

It's not Advertising vs Word of Mouth. It's Advertising x Word of Mouth. Just advertising is wasting money.

Chalo Bulawa Aaya Hai

Neeraj Basur

Most people carry memories and anecdotes from their visits to the holy shrine of Shri Mata Vaishno Devi[1] at Katra, Jammu. Nestled in the Trikuta Mountains, the Vaishno Mata shrine is at an altitude of 5,200 ft above sea level. Devotees believe that one cannot possibly have 'Darshan ' of Mata (The Goddess) unless she herself calls them over to her shrine. The eternal chant 'Chalo

---

[1] A much revered temple of goddess

bulawa aaya hai, Mata ne bulaya hai[2]', means, 'Let us go to Vaishno Devi as Mata has beckoned us to come for her Darshan and Blessings' is therefore, deeply revered among all pilgrims and devotees.

It was a late Sunday afternoon in the September of 1998. My wife and I were generally chatting about visiting the shrine. Both of us had never visited Vaishno Devi shrine before that. We were in Chandigarh at that time. I looked at the next set of approaching holidays and found that Dussehra[3] holiday was at the beginning of October. We thought It was perfect timing to plan this visit. At that time, we had only one son who was then three years old.

As our program began to unfold, my wife's cousin also indicated her inclination to join us. So the plan was made, we decided to drive down to Katra (the starting point of the 13 km trek to the Bhawan) from Chandigarh.

A year back, I had just purchased my first car, a white Maruti 800. So the thrill of driving through a hitherto uncharted terrain was quite palpable. I got inputs from friends at work on the driving route since in 1998 it was still early days for the Internet and 'Google Maps' were not in vogue. One had to rely on the route information from someone or buy a physical route map.

The driving route I was advised to take was Chandigarh – Mohali – Balachaur – Hoshiarpur – Pathankot – Jammu

---

[2]Come visit the holy shrine and see her idol
[3]The festival of Lord Rama's victory over Ravana

– Katra. While there was no issue with the route plan, I was informed that Katra was around 250 Kms or so from Chandigarh. A fact I neither checked nor did I buy a physical map to familiarise myself with the route.

We started our journey on the designated day, full of excitement. Driving through the hinterland of Punjab was quite a pleasing experience with lush fields of the yellowish flowered mustard crop all along the way.

There was, however, one small glitch. The distance between Chandigarh and Katra turned out to be nearly 400 km! Therefore, while we thought we would be able to cover the expected journey of 250 km in around five-to-six hours, it took us close to eight hours to reach our destination.

It was going to be first in the series of learning from this trip.

Tired from the long road journey, we reached our destination late in the evening and checked into hotel Asia Vaishno Devi at Katra. We decided to start our trek to the shrine in the morning.

The plan sounded great, except that it was Dussehra, a holiday, and we had not anticipated the huge rush of pilgrims to descend at Katra. Next morning, after breakfast, the hotel informed us that we needed to procure Yatra Slips (journey passes) from the office of the Shrine Board before we could start our trek.

We were not aware of the process that one had to follow to get the journey passes.

Our second big challenge was awaiting us.

As it was a holiday and there was a heavy rush of pilgrims, the queue for obtaining Yatra Slips was more than 2 km long. We had no choice but to join the serpentine queue. After jostling for close to four hours in the crowd, I managed somehow, to get the passes. The experience of struggling for our turn and getting pushed and shoved around in the crowd was quite humbling for a 'white collard' company executive like me. I managed the passes, and I was already exhausted even before starting the trek.

As we embarked on our journey, we got our three-year-old to firmly plant on a 'Pithoo' ride. A pithoo is someone who carries infants and luggage on their back. Three of us started our fascinating trek. Since it was our first trip, we took our own sweet time to cover the 13 km climb, with few really steep stretches.

For a first-timer, the trek to the shrine can be very tiring and exhausting. Body aches, cramps and stiffened muscles are par for the course. However, the scenic beauty of the Trikuta Mountains and the exuberance & enthusiasm of the pilgrims, all the way chanting, singing and dancing, somewhat mellowed the pain and effort to reach the destination. On the way, we found groups of unknown people urging us to chant 'Jor se bolo', 'Jai Mata Di', energising the atmosphere.

By the time we reached the Bhawan, the place where one enters the Sanctum Sanctorum (the Holy Cave) it was almost 7 pm, and the place was overflowing with pilgrims. Due to the massive holiday rush, the entry to the cave was regulated, and people were being let go in batches. We also got our passes stamped with a designated batch number.

We were about to get jolted one more time. To our dismay, we realised that with more batches waiting ahead of us, our batch was most likely to be allowed entry after some 15 hours of waiting, or even more!

We were in a real fix.

Early in October, the hills of Katra get quite cold in the evening. We had a three-year-old with us. We did carry light woollens with us but by no means were we sufficiently prepared to brave the cold, windy night. With barely enough place to sit down comfortably, we were grappling with the situation. We had a whole night and a half-day ahead of us to wait in the open. We debated if we should wait or return without completing the pilgrimage? It wasn't helping that we were utterly exhausted and unprepared for this ordeal.

Our mood was sombre, and the tiring experience of the day was beginning to take its toll. The temperature dropped to sub 10 degrees. We somehow managed to find seating space on a bench, and the wait began. As the evening progressed, the chill in the wind started to bite. It was clear we were hardly prepared for it.

Shivering due to intense cold and fatigued from the day's events, we did not know what to do next. Our son was getting quite uncomfortable and restless. Having come all the way, we had no choice but to sit there in the open and wait for our turn. The wait was going to be a long one. We wondered whether we truly got a Bulawa (calling/invitation) from Mata (the goddess) or were we being tested by her for our resolve?

Around midnight, something interesting happened.

From literally nowhere, two boys approached us. They had pass for ten people and that three from their group had dropped off earlier in the day. They asked us whether we would want to accompany them as they could accommodate us in their batch, which was almost ready to be ushered in for the Darshan!

It was quite a strange coincidence. Here, we were waiting helplessly, and these boys spotted our plight among so many other pilgrims. It indeed was a 'Bulawa'; a God sent invitation. We were destined to complete our pilgrimage without any further tribulations. The mood suddenly became jubilant.

Was it our sheer luck or was it divine intervention?

We couldn't have asked for more. With renewed energy, vigour and enthusiasm, we were ready for the last mile of our journey. Having thanked our stars and the group of boys profusely, we got into the queue with them.

The atmosphere inside the Holy Cave was quite exhilarating and energising. Goddess Mata Vaishnavi sits there in the form of a five and a half feet rock with three heads or the Pindies on the top. The experience and final sighting inside the Holy Cave was truly mesmerising.

It took us another four hours to trek downhill and reach our hotel. It was early morning. We were up the whole night.

We rested for some time. As we were delayed, there was no choice but to start the return journey by noon on the same day. Driving back after the tiring experience with hardly any rest was another experience for me. With stiffened calf muscles, it wasn't easy to drive. The return journey took us more than 12 hours.

I kept getting drowsy with fatigue and had to stop a couple of times to catch up on some sleep. It dawned on me much after that it was a dangerous drive. With me sleepy behind the wheels, anything was possible. Anyhow, we reached Chandigarh late in the night, and our eventful trip came to an end.

This trip taught me the value and importance of planning and validation.

If only I had done my homework and groundwork on the journey, known about the festival rush of pilgrims, I could have prevented a lot of hassles that we went through. The other key lesson learnt was never to drive long distance when fatigued. It's for one's safety.

The unexpected help we got in the middle of the night from a set of strangers who we will never meet reinforced my belief in humanity and underscored the value of empathy. I learnt a lot about the positive impact that can be made by helping someone. Having been a recipient of a stranger's generosity, I now look out for similar opportunities where I can help and support someone.

This learning episode positively affected my view and opinion of the impact and potential of selfless help.

For the last 12 years, we have been visiting Vaishno Devi every year. The family firmly believes - you complete the holy ritual of Darshan, only when there is a divine beckoning, Her Bulawa.

It's All About Etiquette

Prabhakar Mundkur

August 1989. It was still the days before liberalisation. I had been on the Hindustan Lever account for over 2 years now. We were on a flight from Chennai to Calcutta. Suddenly, I was told that Shunu Sen (the much loved and respected Marketing Director at Hindustan Lever who went on to become Vice Chairman at Lipton), wanted to sit next to me on the flight, so I should catch up with him at the airport. I found that strange. Why would he? However, there had to be a good reason. Shunu was extremely fond of me. He had once said 'fantastic presentation' and then added, 'I normally don't compliment men with a cheeky smile.'

We had just had a great launch conference for International Lux the night before. It was an important conference considering, SM Datta, the Chairman of Hindustan Lever, had decided to grace the occasion with his presence. It went off well, in spite of some really bad hitches with the projection system. These were the days when we still hadn't mastered back projection, and things could still go wrong, especially in cities outside Mumbai. This projector was still showing a straight image but wouldn't work for back projection. Randhir Behl himself was with me at the conference - trying hard to fix a tech problem with the projector. My mathematical brain had figured out that the image had to flip twice over for back projection left to right and bottom to top. Then, when seen from the front from the audience point of view, the image would be right. But of course these were the days of screwdriver technology, and I didn't know anything about electronics. I had learnt from my dad to just kick the radio to make it work. Nevertheless, minutes before the Chairman came in, the projector decided to behave itself, and the show went on fabulously.

Finally, we were in the plane. Shunu was courteous as usual. Not giving me a clue about why he wanted me to sit next to him on the aircraft. I was dreading it in many ways. I just loved him and admired him as a client. In fact, he was a role model. But then he was senior. And I wasn't still sure that I would want to spend two and a half hours with him in an aircraft. The flight took off, and we were airborne. Shunu asked me if I would have some beer. That was a bit of a surprise. These were the days when you could carry your own liquor on Indian Airlines, a privilege that you don't have today on local flights. When the pilot announced that we were at 30,000 feet, Shunu pulled out some chilled beer cans. I noticed it was Heineken. Heineken in 1989, in a still to be liberalised India. My eyes lit up at the thought of starting the day with Heineken, but in many ways, this was going to be the longest flight I had ever taken. Longer than the two and a half hours it was supposed to take.

After a few sips, I had a premonition about what was coming. Shunu was angry with me. And he wanted to pulverise me on this two and a half hour flight to Calcutta. In many ways, this was the worst firing I had in my life. Never had it even happened with my own bosses back at the agency. He was angry because I hadn't shown him the advertising presentation that I made so well at the Chennai launch conference. I had never seen him so angry. I explained that I had shown it to his Marketing Manager. His point was that I was presenting in the presence of his Chairman (SM Datta) and how dare I not show him my presentation for approval. Well, he had a point. Nevertheless, I just thought that his Marketing

Manager was taking charge of the show, and if at all Shunu had to see the presentation, he would show it to him. But the words that really stayed with me for the rest of my life were something else. Shunu ended this toxic conversation (beer and anger) by using two words that stuck with me for the rest of my life. He told me that he thought I was extremely well-behaved and, just as we follow etiquettes in our personal lives, we must make sure we follow protocols in our corporate life. He spoke and used the words 'corporate etiquette'. And according to corporate etiquette, I was rude to him the previous evening. I had no defense.

Shunu then quietened down, and the rest of the flight was spent in pleasantries. I could once again enjoy my Heineken beer. And I knew he really liked me, and I was one of his favourite advertising executives.

How Corporate Etiquette affects our lives.

That conversation with Shunu made an impact on me forever. It was so impressionable that forever after that I would classify events and other people's behaviours as good corporate etiquette and bad corporate etiquette. It somehow made me realise how important it was for corporations to be well behaved. And I decided that I was going to be the apostle of good corporate etiquette wherever I went.

Once the idea of corporate etiquette as being important is firmly entrenched in your mind, it changes your attitude to things around you in the workplace. When you are senior, people often imitate your behaviour. And if you believe in good corporate etiquette, you can be sure that people around will also follow business courtesies.

If a senior person was leaving and even if my company wouldn't foot the bill (the last company I worked for wouldn't), I made sure I would throw a send-off party for the man at my own cost. Or I would get a few senior colleagues to share the cost. If nothing else, I would call him home for dinner. I think people who are leaving your company, must still always think kindly of their time there. An employee is still your brand ambassador, even after he has given up working for you. Many companies don't quite get that. And even if you have given an employee a pink slip, you must treat him well before he goes. The relationship must continue to be cordial.

Only recently, I went to see a very senior ex-client at their offices. As it so happened, we had parted company many years ago. She was forced to sack our agency because her boss had sued my boss on some financial transaction they had, which was not related to our client-agency relationship. (One of those unfortunate experiences, when bosses decide to do business with each other at a personal level, and it doesn't work out). However, I was pleasantly surprised when I reached the reception. I wasn't treated like any other ordinary guest. My client's assistant was there at the reception to greet me and walk me up the elevator right to the client's cabin. I was almost embarrassed. However, it made me feel very special. That's good etiquette. I was being respected for my seniority in the industry. When I reached my client's cabin, I got a warm and affectionate hug.

The other day I met a friend of mine who used to be a client, and he told me about an incident that I thought was good corporate etiquette. As a client, he had a 5-year relationship with one of his agencies, but the time had come for fresher thinking and to part ways. I believe he threw a send-off party for his agency. The agency was surprised. And the parting was still a happy parting. I think that is really good corporate etiquette. I have been sacked many times just over coffee and a parting letter terminating the agreement. It is unlikely that I am going to say good things about that company in the future.

Some people may disagree with me, but the best people I have met in corporate life knew their etiquette. They were always well-mannered. It is something that carries forward from your personal life into your corporate life. Somehow I can't help feeling that if one wants to get ahead in corporate life, it is not enough to just have ambition. To be a well -rounded senior corporate executive who can be respected, you must be well mannered in the workplace; as well-mannered as you are when you are home with your friends and family.

As Goethe said 'A man's manners are a mirror in which he shows his own portrait.'

When Things Go Right

Sanhita Baruah

I rubbed my eyes with my fingers as tears of tiredness ran down my cheek. One of the men of the office-cleaning service, in his black-and-white uniform, picked up the empty cup of coffee from my desk as I stared at the screen of my office desktop.

My shoulder-length hair was carelessly tied in a shapeless bun, showing signs of not been combed in the last 24 hours. My eyebrows grew past the phase of needing threading, and in the last few days, I forgot to apply kajal on my eyes. I remember, later that year, one of my team leads, Dona once said to me, 'At least wear a pair of earrings or tops.'

'Coming for lunch?' my friend and a senior colleague, Kunal, the 25-year old Gujarati famous for bringing khakras for the team, asked me as he passed by my desk to walk to the cafeteria.

'Naah. I'll pass,' I said and brought my attention back to typing the code I was working on.

There's hardly any parallel to the amount of enthusiasm a new joinee brings into their work at an organisation. It was 2014, and I was barely five months old at Capgemini India Pvt. Ltd., my first workplace after just graduating from college.

'Working so hard, eh?' the tech-savvy friend and colleague, Venkat asked me when he came back from lunch.

'Yeah, that's because I am going to submit this Unit Case Test Results document ahead of everyone else,' I replied with a mix of arrogance and excitement.

Later that day, I stayed back when most others left the office at around 9:00 pm.

It was the second iteration of my project at work, and after learning from the horrible mistakes I made in the previous one- the chaotic first-time-for-everyone iteration, I was almost walking on eggshells this time, too determined to be visibly better, too hard-headed on doing things right.

There's something about doing things well ahead of the deadlines that beats all other ways of being satisfied by one's productivity.

When it was half an hour until midnight, I decided I had worked enough to go home to sleep.

I had joined as a Guidewire developer in one of the new projects of the company at Mumbai, once I had graduated from the 3-months long induction program. I had ten other batch-mates from the induction program in my project as my friends and competitors – same age group, same job position, and same appraisal cycle.

A new project in the insurance domain required not only a lot of work but a lot of understanding of the business as well. Hence, our working hours began at 11 in the morning but ended as long as the day could go.

The next day, after spending a tiring Wednesday, I made sure to have mailed all the completed documents before I left office.

'Any bottlenecks, guys?' the team lead, Srinath Sir (No, the habit of using 'Sir' and 'Madam' hadn't subsided by then) asked at the end of the stand-up meeting the next morning.

The answer was usually no from my side unless there were some requirements or approvals pending from the on-site. That day I had only a few more tests to run on my code – just one more excel sheet to fill, and I'd be free for rest of the week.

Aastha, the one with the dark curly hair and large beautiful eyes, expressed a few of her concerns at first. She was known for her sincerity even during our three-months-long induction program back in Hyderabad. There were a couple of more issues placed by the rest of the team of 12 developers in the project before the meeting was concluded.

As soon as we dispersed to our seats, I caught a glimpse of Gourav, another of the ten batch-mates, approaching one of the team leads, Arulraj Sir (because the old habit of 'sir'-ing someone doesn't die easily). Gourav was a thin 25-year old Punjabi guy, who was one of the top contenders for the best employee award, an apple of every manager's eye. I saw them sitting together for hours that day.

I remember approaching Arulraj Sir only once when I couldn't find how to make a dynamic title bar in the Guidewire Help documents, mostly because I was looking for the word 'dynamic' which wasn't the adjective the documents contained. I remember him handling my queries patiently, briefly obliterating my fears of seeming too pestering to seniors – one of the reasons why I avoided seeking help from people and kept most of my technical queries to the help-documents instead. However, the college-girl within me remained intact who'd try not to ask unnecessary questions to professors when the answers could be explored some other way.

So, before asking any queries to our on-site counterparts working from the US, I looked into the help documents of

Guidewire, for that was the tool I was customising for our clients, for the answers.

Also, the need to be appreciated for my work made me attempt to work efficiently. So, I bothered people less; my calls were shorter. My doubts regarding requirements, if any, were simply mailed and answered to; I was so proud of myself.

That evening when I talked to my on-site senior, Amol, I promised my work would be finished by the next morning. Our telephonic meetings with the on-site seniors usually happened at 7 in the evening. As I chose documents over people, my call was a short one that hardly lasted half an hour leaving me free to finish my pending work items that evening itself.

I finished my excel sheet and all other pending items at around 9 p.m. and ascended the staircase to have dinner in the office cafeteria before calling it a day.

When I returned from the cafeteria after having a filling meal of roti and bhindi masala at around half past eight o' clock, I saw Gourav still clutching the earpiece of his telephone. The next day I realised that the conversation with his on-site senior went until midnight.

'Sanhita, are you free for today?' Srinath Sir asked me when he saw that I was doing nothing but enjoying my cup of coffee the next morning.

'Yes. I've submitted all my deliverables for the week,' I claimed with a grin on my face.

And before I could dip another biscuit in my coffee, he replied gesturing at me to look at the screen of his laptop.

'Well then, here's some other work you might want to your shift your attention to.'

I couldn't believe that I had to do more work just because I finished things before time. I was under the heavenly assumption that finishing work fast meant no work for the rest of the day.

Later in the day when we had a quick status-update meeting, Srinath Sir congratulated Gourav for having solved a problem that he was stuck with for the last few days. While an abashed Gourav smiled at the praise, I wondered why I did not receive any appreciation.

It's difficult to understand at first that unlike college I don't have to only do well in the exams and score great. The scoring in real life and workplaces is probably a product of one's entire lifetime there, the total process from the beginning to the end.

However, I could not recollect where I went wrong. There was no way I was going to get the best employee award. I could foresee it. All the nights and days I worked so hard suddenly seemed meaningless to me.

As I worked on the new requirements Srinath Sir gave me that morning, I took some time to contemplate if I could still make things better. I typed a line of code repeatedly as I wondered how influential leaders like Steve Jobs become who they are now.

Having always been influenced by people who have overcome their hardships, bringing to the world stories of struggle to tell, with a happy ending, I wondered what my work-life would appear to a reader if it were a story.

My appraisers, my managers, would be the readers of my work-life who would see only parts of the entire story- excerpts that I choose to make them read. Was I even making them read the germane excerpts? Or were there no excerpts that they could read, at all?

I stopped re-typing the code to review the challenges I had faced in writing the code at the first place – I had referred a few documents, worked out a few other ways to see which one works the best, takes the least time, and looks the shortest too.

I had probably done my very best for the project, crossed a few hurdles, but there was no story that my readers could read for I always was the character whose name would be mentioned in a book, but only as the person who just passes by the protagonist.

I looked at the larger picture of Steve Jobs on the whiteboard of another employee sitting a few desks away from my office space, wondering what made him stand out.

If Steve Jobs became so famous and was worshipped only because Apple's performance dwindled post his resignation in 1985, and, when he returned in 1997, he salvaged the brand, taking it to newer heights, I wondered, where was such a downfall in my story before the reader? If

I am inspired only by the struggles people have overcome, where was my brand resurgence?

It was then that enlightenment happened.

I realised that when things went right in my scope of work, they actually went wrong for me as a professional person.

A job well done is expected, not rewarded; what's noteworthy is when you face a problem, work on it, find a solution and emerge as a hero. And when there is not much of a problem faced or talked about, there's hardly any area of improvement expected by the leadership.

As if confirming to my thoughts, I heard Srinath Sir talking about the same with another team member as both walked past me on the way to the cafeteria.

'People hardly care when things are going right. It's when things go wrong that you're noticed amidst a crowd of hundred,' Srinath Sir added in his speech as he looked at me and gave a smile of approval.

Strength Of Character Defines You

Vikas Mehta

One of the things I realised earlier on in my career was the importance of man management. In my initial years as a junior, I made it a habit of picking up negative and positive traits of my bosses, resolving what I will do and what I will never do to my subordinates. It helped me a lot in my later years as I tried dealing with my juniors the way I expected my seniors to treat me.

But advertising is also a challenging business and every day throws new challenges in terms of man management. And one of my toughest challenges came pretty late in my career and in an unexpected way.

I was heading the profit centre of one of India's well-known advertising agencies, with a large team reporting to me, directly or indirectly. I would not be hands-on with everyone but would definitely be a part of the assessment and appraisal of every member of my team. Similarly, for new hires, I would delegate it to my team members but would meet each selected candidate before signing off on any recruitment. So I was clued in on almost everyone in the team and had a fair sense of every team member's strength and weakness.

One morning our studio manager, let's call him PK, studio being a common source for all teams and hence the studio manager was important to all teams, called me and requested a one to one meeting immediately. I sensed that something was seriously out of line.

Sure enough, PK came with a troubling issue. One of his artists, a few days ago had bought an expensive smartphone. And the evening before the phone had gone missing in the studio. As it was late in the evening, not many people were in the studio, and a quick look at the security cameras revealed the disappearance of the phone, which was lying on the artist's table, after the exit of a young fresh account executive of my group from the studio. It was indeed not conclusive proof, but the circumstantial evidence pointed to him. Let's call this guy Joe.

To make matters worse, the phone locator revealed the phone to be near the metro station where Joe lived. Further, when they had called him at night, he had acknowledged that he was home. On being questioned about the phone, he had denied knowing anything about it. And minutes after the conversation, the phone had been switched off.

PK, who himself was a 15-year industry veteran, had come to me having done all the above homework. It seemed to be an open and shut case, but he wanted to talk to me about it first before reporting about it to HR. Actually, he was quite shocked, as he had taken a liking for Joe.

Joe had been with us for about seven months. He was diligent, soft-spoken, a keen learner, handled pressure well, and there was no one who had anything wrong to say about him. I called in Joe's immediate boss and taking him into confidence asked him what he felt about the incident.

He was also shocked but concurred that the circumstantial evidence was too substantial to ignore. Here was a youngster who was good at his work, had a positive attitude and got along well with everyone, but seemingly had an ethical problem. I could have easily handed over the case to HR, who would have taken the appropriate action, resulting in the guy's sacking.

But this was the first time me, or PK or even Joe's boss had a negative comment against Joe. Joe's boss was refusing to believe that he was capable of doing such a thing. And his astonishment was genuine. My intuition took over from there.

Even though we had no direct evidence, I called Joe, and without mincing any words, I accused him of the robbery. And before he could react I ticked him off for breaching our trust in him. He sat quietly with his face down. It was apparent that he had done the act. I offered him an easy way out. I asked him to leave the phone on my desk in my absence, along with his resignation letter, and we would not pursue the matter further. That would have been his saving face.

He didn't say a word, nodded and left my room.

About half an hour later, PK, along with the studio artist, came to my room. Joe had gone to the artist, handed over the phone to him, apologised and asked for his forgiveness. And then he had left the office. Both PK and the artist were so taken in by this gesture that they had come to me asking me to be lenient with Joe!!!!

I was stunned. This youngster had shown character. He had erred with a fatal lapse of judgement but had then rebounded back by owning up manfully and taking it on in the best possible way. Suddenly my attitude towards Joe had changed.

Joe, by this one gesture, had demonstrated a very rare trait of holding himself responsible for his actions. There were no excuses, no laments, no asking for one more chance. He had redeemed himself by his affirmative action.

Now, I was in a dilemma. Until now my mind was made up that Joe had to go. Lifting stuff from a colleague was just not on. Frankly, till then my dilemma was about how to fix the blame firmly on Joe, as we had only circumstantial evidence and no concrete proof. But now this incident had shown the strength of character of Joe. This guy knew how to pick himself off the floor and bounce back.

By then, HR had got a whiff about the incident. The HR head came to me and asked me point blank about the whole matter. I told her everything. Her response was quite similar to my initial response. This guy gave into temptation and had committed a crime. He had to go. And not go quietly but had to be made an example. And now that he had confessed, we did not need to bother about the niceties too. I apparently had a lot of convincing to do.

I first called Joe. He was contrite and apologetic. He said that he was ready for any punishment, but he had definitely learnt his lesson. I then called PK and the artiste whose phone had been stolen. They were too happy to let the matter go. The artiste kept on saying that Joe had more than compensated by coming back and returning the phone personally. He made a mistake but had now atoned for it, and we should just forget the matter.

I took all the parties to the HR head. She was sympathetic but wanted to play by rules. Her stance was that this was a criminal offence and grave enough to warrant a police complaint. The best she could do was to let Joe resign and leave peacefully without any black mark against his name. But there was no way that he would be allowed to remain on company rolls. Besides she had already discussed the matter with the HR chief in Mumbai, who was also clear that Joe had to go.

Now, I had two options. The first was to agree with the HR people and let Joe leave. After all, his initial misdemeanour was severe enough. And the second was to escalate the matter with my boss at a national level as I seriously thought that the HR was being too straight-jacketed by the rule book and was losing out on an excellent opportunity to show its employee-friendly face.

So I chose the third route. I spoke to the HR boss and my boss, and after briefing them on the case, I let them know that we could use this case to showcase the importance of strength of character and how as an organisation we actually value such skills. The idea was to make this incident into a case study of sorts. And the only way to do that would be for the organisation also to show that it does not play by the book every time and is open to looking at each case of misdemeanour with an open mind.

In most companies and especially in advertising agencies, HR is always seen as a top management appendage, which is a hiring and firing department with a bit of training programmes thrown in between. This incident handled properly, could show HR in a good light. After a few more discussions and arguments, finally, the management agreed not to fire Joe. The tricky part now was to leverage it positively without hurting the sensibilities of Joe.

As it happens in most of these cases, it is difficult to keep a lid on such incidents. I realised that the whole office was in the know of the incident. Joe came to me asking me to stop making an effort to keep him back as he felt that he would never be trusted in the organisation any more.

But by now, I was determined to ensure two things. One, a moment's indiscretion should not cost a youngster his career, and two, I wanted to showcase how strength of character can actually be a powerful trait that can eliminate friction between two people.

So, I organised a small event. I got my team as well as the full studio team along with the HR people to assemble during lunchtime in the conference room. After a small preamble of 2 minutes, I called on Joe to speak. Joe spoke for barely a minute, mumbling his apologies and accepting any punishment. But it was PK and the artiste who stole the show. They both quickly embraced Joe. The studio manager praised Joe and lauded him for his strength in acknowledging his fault, knowing fully well the repercussions. He also declared that no one should judge Joe by his one mistake, but he should be judged by his stint in the organisation. Two more senior members in my team chipped in and spoke about how they had never seen anybody in their long experience have the guts to not only acknowledge grave misjudgement but also to be strong enough to face his victim. And finally, the HR head also gave a small supportive speech.

By now the mood in the room had turned into a celebratory one. Everyone was appreciative of Joe. Initially, I had thought that I would conclude the event with another motivational spiel. But the mood was so positively infectious that I refrained from doing so.

The bottom line was that Joe carried on. He had become a more loyal employee than ever. Everyone felt good about the organisation. HR came off in a good light, and many understood how strength of character could make or break a person.

Never underestimate the power of your character. It defines you.

A Girl On The Highway

Sanhita Baruah

'Is there a PCO nearby?'

The old man, wearing his dirty white *kurta* and *dhoti* looked at me as if he was not only surprised by but also dubious of what I asked him. He needed the help of his walking stick to walk while he stroked his long curly white beard with his free hand- a hand that showed signs of ageing, of having worked hard its entire life.

I, taken aback, took a second to figure if I uttered the abbreviation of a Public Call Office correctly.

It's interesting how the term PCO, so common in the previous decade, has been completely obliterated from our minds in this one. I too wouldn't have even thought of a PCO had I not been completely alone, stranded in a suburb, near an almost empty highway without my Smartphone. Had it been a dark evening and somewhere near Delhi, I'd have been worried out of my wits.

However, it was only somewhere near Kharghar in Navi Mumbai on a sunny November afternoon. And the only living being near me, apart from the dirt-covered grass losing its greenery, was the old man who just happened to pass by with a flock of goats.

I was 23 then, dressed in a pink shirt, a pair of black jeans and the shoes I used to wear while appearing for all my important examinations in those years. The important examination was the Common Admission Test (CAT) that day, and all I wanted was to return home to discuss the questions with my friends.

In an era where our eyes are constantly hooked up on the smartphones in our hands, my only phone had decided to give up on me just that morning, acting haywire as I dressed myself for the day. I had some hundred rupees in my pocket; and when my friend, Sanketh had dropped me off at the other side of the highway in the morning, in our hurry, we had forgotten to decide where to meet while returning.

After my exam was over, as I walked out from the residential area towards the highway, I had made a call from the phone of a stranger- a teenager wearing a checked cap to match with her pony-tailed hair, a royal blue linen top and a grey skirt, who had stopped looking at the *selfie* she just clicked. She was just walking into a CCD[1] near my examination hall, when I asked for her phone to inform Sanketh that I'd be on the highway in the opposite side of 'just where you left me.'

It was only when I walked along the highway trying to search for landmarks to figure out 'just where' he had dropped me. I realized the highway was vast and too nondescript.

It was difficult to tell one spot from the other in the highway arca. My walk on it was more tiring and time-taking than I had imagined, and I had absolutely no clue where to go. After all, in the morning after getting off the bike, I had to stray off to check out various roads to eventually find the exam centre- all that without the guidance of my phone's GPS.

So there I was, at 2 in the day, when the shutters of the only three shops near that part of the highway were shut on the grounds of lunch-break, waiting for someone to come along on his Hero Honda CBZ, without even knowing if he'd be able to guess where exactly I was.

---

[1]Cafe Coffee Day

I badly needed a phone in that area devoid of people, with occasional vehicles passing me by in full speed, a smartphone with lost marbles in one hand and a handkerchief soaked in my sweat in another.

I kept on meandering near a certain part of the highway I decided could be the opposite side of the spot where we had parted ways. The flock of goats and the goatherd were gone by now, and the purple Fastrack watch on my hand said 2.55pm – still no sign of my friend.

It was when I was about to give up waiting for my friend and to go home by myself, leaving him to probably keep searching for me (had he not given up already) that I saw two men who got off a long-distance bus a little farther from where I stood. It didn't take me many seconds to decide to start walking towards them in search of a phone.

My feet perspired inside my shoes as I walked towards them- their chassis growing larger with each step of mine. When I was around 15 metres away from them, it dawned on me that there was no chance that they could be the saviours of my situation.

They were two extremely thin and dark men probably in their late twenties – both with dishevelled clothes and oiled red hair that showed signs of being black once. Their appearances somehow reminded me of the tiny patches of grass near the highway – feeble and covered with dirt.

One of them wore a bright orange, wrinkled and torn-at-places shirt I'd never pick for someone if I were going shopping. The other wore a rumpled yellow T-shirt that had lost its yellowness years ago, as if complimenting his companion, and kept combing his neck-length oiled hair with his long and thin fingers. Both wore brown trousers smeared at places with what looked like black shoe-polish.

They seemed to be people I'd have effortlessly warded off in a busy street in Mumbai, people not earning well enough to have a day's proper meal. They also seemed to be people I'd be scared of if the sun had set by then.

Being alone on a highway, without a phone, with only two such people around was a situation I thought I'd never want myself to be in again.

The consequences of any of my actions could range from anything to anything, judging by the news reports we hear every other day. There are chances you don't want to take at all, in a world where you're a girl often burdened with the worries of your family members and loved ones, every time you go out alone.

Amidst all the thinking of negative consequences, another dilemma was whether to unintentionally hurt someone else's feeling in the guise of a call for help. Asking them for a phone to make a call would have been nothing but demeaning to them.

After putting some thought into it, I dropped the risky idea of asking for help from the strangers; I ceased to walk towards them to stand there awaiting my friend's arrival, subsiding my impatience.

As another fifteen minutes elapsed, I decided to cease the over-analysis and try my luck one more time.

So I, despite all the hesitations, approached the man in orange, the one with the shorter hair who looked a tad better off than the other. As I walked towards him, I wished I were not so desperate to act so insensitive.

In a tone as polite as I could act, I hid my helplessness as I asked, '*Bhaiya*[2], would you, by any chance, be carrying a mobile phone? I need to make a call.'

Unlike the questions asked to the girl I had previously borrowed a phone from, near the residential area, this question of mine did not assume that the other person could definitely have a phone. The 'could I borrow your phone' question was no longer valid in my mind.

He looked at me with eyes that questioned my existence in that area; he shook his head.

I was almost losing all my hopes of making a call when he opened his mouth to speak,' I don't have a phone. Nevertheless, my tab has calling facilities. Would you want to use it?'

It is not important how and when I reached home that day. The crucial words still ringing in my ears are what he said, '*Phone nahi hai. Par mere tab se call ho sakta hai, Chalega?*'

I wasn't only embarrassed for having assumed his financial capabilities just by looking at him but I also felt

---

[2]Brother

naïve for making the wrong judgment, for not having considered even once that they could have a phone or a tab.

Prejudice is something we all wish to avoid when it comes to preaching to others while unknowingly we, often a time, are ourselves the victims of judgments we frame in our minds.

'I am an open-minded person,' we claim in our conversations and speeches but fail to practice when it comes to the realities of life.

More than a year later when it was my turn to conduct a research on consumer consumption patterns for my internship at Hindustan Coca-Cola Beverages, this incident reminded me to leave those prejudices aside.

I didn't just look at a person on the street and consider them fit or unfit for my premium category product. I'd talk to them, observe their buying behaviour in a mall, analyze their answers for various questions and then decide whether they could be within our target group or not.

I studied the Bangalore market, a city where I was visiting for the first time, a city very different from the current city I live in – Gurgaon. And hence, there was bound to be a culture bias.

While talking to my co-interns regarding consumer analysis I'd notice the assumptions they have in mind based on the appearances – either for a shop or for a consumer. However, when it comes to market research and assessment, one of the key things we learn in our Research Methods in Business classes is to attempt to remove the biases the interviewer creates.

If anything that incident of panic taught me, it was to leave my prejudices at home, not only for my professional work but also my personal relationships.

One of the students at MDI whom others considered useless turns out to be one of the toppers in the college. A lady with the least sense of fashion, with her unkempt hair, instead of turning out to be a subordinate at my previous workplace, turns out to be a senior manager. One humble person wearing a plain T-shirt and a simple pair of trousers turn out to be the CEO of an international firm. A person wearing a stained sweatshirt, eating at the road-side *dhaba* turns out to be a highly-paid consultant with a car I could never afford when I was working. And a knowledgeable man talking to me about the culture differences in the various countries of Europe, wearing an ironed US Polo T-shirt turns out to be a cab driver.

Once I remove the barriers I create, once I have a conversation with the other person without prejudices, I realize there is so much to learn from so many people; there are revelations at times, at other times, there is an absolute delight.

Sardar Khush Hoga

Sanjeev Kotnala

It is almost dark inside the room. The Seven Samurais are standing in a single file. They are facing the desk of the Don[1], the Gabbar[2], of the organisation.

The situation is tense. At the end of today, a new travel policy will came into operation in Mudra.

---

[1]Expert gangster played by Amitabh Bachchan in the movie by the same name and later played by Shahrukh Khan in the remake.

[2]One of the most liked and feared, iconic and immortalised villains in Indian Cinema

So, what happened?

It is the very first year of my career in advertising. After completing my PGDM from IIM Ahmedabad and three-month rigorous training under 'Mudra Management Training Programme, ' I am finally at ground Zero. I am at Manikamm Apartment, the Headquarters and the Ahmedabad branch office of Mudra.

Mayur Fabrics is one of the clients I service. Their headquarters is at Gulabpura, Bhilwara, where Mr. Laddhajee, the Marketing Director sits.

To meet the client, I take the evening train to Ajmer. From there a cab, which invariably is a white Ambassador and drive down some 80 km to Gulabpura. Such travel needs mean that the client meetings are mostly scheduled well in advance.

The account is not big. However, it is as dear to AGK as any other account of Mudra. AGK takes pride in what Mudra deliveres and hence client satisfaction is one of the critical parameter.

....

It is Tuesday when the client calls. At that time, I am the only client servicing person in the office and on the account. It requires me to take charge and to act like the senior most team member. The client wants to see the winter campaign on Friday. The deadline is non-negotiable. The presentation is, anyway, much delayed. It is another thing that the campaign was still to be initiated at the agency.

It is too much of a pressure for a raw junior like me. However, I decide to rise to the occasion. I ask Jayesh Bhai and Philip in the creative department for help. They agree to do rough layouts that I can present to the client.

It seems a smart solution. This way, I will have honoured the client's request and bought time to create and present the real campaign.

Finally, the campaign is ready. Not the best, but we all agree it was okay for the initial presentation. On Thursday night, I take the train to Ajmer. I am alone. There is no senior in town to join me on my adventure.

....

I am back in Ahmedabad on Saturday. I think the meeting went Okay.

There is no hint of what was to come next.

Apparently, the MD of Mayur Suitings failed to appreciate our efforts and the campaign. He communicated his feeling along with a few other strong statements to AGK ove FAX. In a nutshell, Don (AGK) in that communication, saw the client questioning Mudra's capabilities to deliver. That is something he hates.

I was unaware of behind the scene happenings.

....

Monday morning, I get a message that AGK has asked me to come down to his big room, I walk in smiling.

He does not ask me to sit. He call the office boy and ask him to get Philip (Art Director), Jayesh (Visualiser), Subrato Bhowmick (Creative Head), Vijay Nagrare (Client Servicing Head), Vijay (Studio Head), Raju Murugesan (Media Head) and Dheeraj Bhai (Production Head). I am not sure, but I think he calls for Allan[3] too.

They all come and take their place in the slowly growing human chain in AGK's room. Being the first one to walk in, I am naturally at the extreme inside corner.

Once satisfied that all are in, AGK starts his monologue.

He wants to know, 'How did the campaign reach the client? Don't we have any quality controls? Who worked on the campaign? Why and how did theu reach the client? Are they aware that the client has sent a nasty fax challenging Mudra creative capabilities? Are we not all ashamed of it?

AGK was firing questions after question. Lack of explanation and answers was making the room heavy. AGK continued for some 30 odd minutes. It seemed like hours to us. I felt as if weight were attached to my feet. My feets were numb. Even if I tried moving them, I failed to do so.

---

[3] Allan was heading the branch, and I am not sure if he was called in for this dressing down

When prompted by AGK, I shared the complete episode. As all the seniors, including him, were out of town, I, the servicing person, took charge of the situation. We crafted a campaign. We all felt it was worth presenting to the client and hence I went and presented it.

AGK immiedeately could see, there was a flaw in the system.

He softened his approach towards me.

The seniors were still on crossfire.

Mudra from then and there got a new polic on travel. It flashed through fax and telex to all the branches.

All seniors from any Mudra office can never be missing from operations at the same time. AGK.

. . . .

The story is not over. Service recovery had to be done. He asked for a fully finished Mudra quality campaign by evening. The session was over. Slowly, everyone left the room. I am the last one.

I too move towards the door, when AGK called for me 'Kotnala'.

My first reaction is 'Now. What have I done?'.

I face AGK, and he asks e a simple question.. WILL YOU DO THIS AGAIN?

I am prompt with my unhesistant reply 'Under similar circumstamces, MAYBE.'

He looks at me and smils. 'Yeah, keep this attitude, you will go a long way'; his hand searches in the drawer of his desk, and he hands me few pieces of Swaad[4].

I smile. I feel relieved of the tension. I slowly step out in the world of newfound wisdom. Sardar Kush Hua.

---

[4]A low- cost, hard-boiled candy during late eighties

Trust Delivered

Neeraj Basur

It was early January of 2007 and a day as usual for me in the Corporate Office at Max India.

My intercom rang, and I could see Ananth's name on the caller ID. B Anantharaman or Ananth as we used to address him was then Joint Managing Director at Max India.

'Neeraj, can I see you please?' Ananth asked.

I walked to his office 5 minutes later and saw him seated on the couch sipping coffee.

'Come, have a seat' he said. I went and took my usual place on the sofa, beside him.

'We are going ahead,' he continued, 'I just had a long conversation on this with Analjit, start preparing and let me have a detailed plan by tomorrow.'

I was equally excited.

I knew what he was talking about. Over the previous six months, we had been deliberating and debating alternative courses of action around raising a substantial amount of capital. We needed money to fund the next round of growth for the highly capital intensive life insurance and healthcare businesses that Max India had nurtured for almost seven years. Our ability to raise the next round of capital would potentially determine and influence the extent of long-term success for both the businesses, which were yearning for a much bigger scale.

Ananth and I had proposed to the Board, the option of raising fresh equity capital through a Qualified Institutional Placement (QIP), which in short meant the public issue of equity shares, meant only for institutional investors. In essence, the rigour and process involved with a QIP are no different than raising capital by way of an Initial Public Offering (IPO), which people are mostly familiar with.

Ananth had just confirmed that our proposal had been accepted, and we were good to move with our proposed QIP. It was going to be an important event for the Group.

The ability of the underlying businesses to grow and create long-term shareholder value was dependent on the success of our initiative. The outcome, as they say, was strategically critical.

I was excited at the prospect of being a part of this journey and to lead the largest QIP by any corporate in India, till then. We were mandated to raise INR 1,000 crore. Our Board had placed a great deal of trust on Ananth, and in turn, he unflinchingly trusted me to deliver on the stated goals.

The process of raising equity capital by a publicly listed company is reasonably complicated and involves simultaneous compliance with multiple regulators. To kick-start the process, we needed to take one major decision. We needed to choose a merchant banker. Companies usually appoint multiple merchant bankers for such large capital raising initiatives. The primary reason is to approach a wider investor base and spread the marketing risk involved with the issue.

Generally, there is a beauty parade of the Merchant Bankers, and the final selection is made based on their track record, reputation with investor groups, commercial competitiveness and so on.

In our case, there was a catch. We had to complete the capital raising project within three months, from start to finish. In early 2007, the capital markets were moving positively. Market timing was apt. We did not intend to miss it. Most critically, the next tranche of capital was required within 90 days. Involving multiple merchant bankers would have meant a more extended preparatory period, potential loss of time and also running the risk of not timing the market.

As a team leader, it was on me to make the critical recommendation of going ahead with a sole merchant banker and also selecting our preferred banker. We did not have the time to go through a beauty parade.

I had been interacting with few people at CLSA[1] over the preceding three years and was impressed by the depth of their relationship with institutional investors. Their research capabilities were well respected by the investor community, and they had handled quite a few solo capital raising projects. I knew, if we had to go with only one merchant banker, it had to be CLSA.

I made the recommendation and could convince Ananth on CLSA being appointed the sole merchant banker for our QIP. He agreed. I knew he completely trusted my judgment, and I had to rally the entire project team to live up to his trust.

We started working in full earnest with the CLSA team led by Pankaj Agarwal, their Managing Director, and

---

[1]Credit Lyonnais Securities Asia is Asia's leading equity brokers and investment group focused on institutional broking, investment banking and asset management to corporate and institutional clients around the world

Nemkumar and Bharat Parajia, who were leading their institutional sales teams.

Little did I know that we were soon going to face severe turbulence.

It was middle of March, some 45 days after the start of the project; I get this call from Pankaj. 'Richard Taylor, our Asia Pac head of investment banking would like to have an urgent con call with you and Ananth, preferably today.'

I instantly knew something was wrong. Pankaj did not sound like his usual chirpy self. My anxiety level peaked.

We spoke with Richard the same evening. He had news to share. Nemkumar and Bharat, who were leading CLSA's institutional sales had decided to quit. Moreover, a few other key executives were going to move. The public announcement was scheduled the same day. Richard wanted to give us an early warning.

Nemkumar and Bharat's relationship with reputed institutional investors was well known, and their skill to woo high-quality investors to subscribe was vital to our success. Their decision to leave CLSA could have serious repercussions for the project success.

I suddenly felt that the rug had been pulled from under our feet.

To assuage our concerns and as a damage control initiative, Richard told us, CLSA as an institution was committed to delivering on our assignment, and they would rally the entire organisation behind our project to ensure a successful closure.

While the assurance was great, I knew Ananth's and my reputation, and credibility was at stake. Ananth completely trusted me on this.

Had we erred in placing all our bets on CLSA?

The reputational damage associated with an unsuccessful capital raising event could prove to be irreparable for the Company.

Failure was not an option.

I had a long, candid chat with Pankaj and Nemkumar. We all agreed to double our collective efforts and deliver on the trust, and the faith reposed on us.

Our challenge was not over yet. There was more to come.

The next day we had company. DLF[2] announced its timetable for its Initial Public Offering (IPO). Our problem was compounded. The timing of DLF's IPO and our QIP overlapped, and it was going to conflict.

There were two potential issues to contend with.

Competing with a company like DLF who was going to approach the same set of institutional investors for a share of their investment wallet was going to be very tough. At the same time, we had the executive exit challenge at CLSA. It meant that due to their impending

---

[2] A premier real estate company in India

exit, Nemkumar and Bharat were to operate under some degree of organisational limitations.

In early 2007, capital market investors were thoroughly fascinated with India's real estate and infrastructure growth story and were lapping up all the investment opportunities served to them. We also knew that institutional investors typically worked within investment exposure limits at each country's level. If they were faced with a choice of investing in two alternate opportunities at the same time, we would surely run the risk of potential rationing of investment, and it could prove to be detrimental for us.

Accordingly, Pankaj and I decided that to enhance our investor reach, the road-show efforts needed to be extensive. Our road-show started in early May of 2007. In order to comprehensively cover the global investors across India, we split ourselves into two teams. While Ananth took charge of investors in North America and Europe, I covered the base in India, Far East and North America.

I was amazed to see the logistical support CLSA teams put behind the scenes.

It was a demonstration of all hands on deck from their side. Overnight, they set up a parallel institutional sales team to work across multiple geographies simultaneously.

Nemkumar and Bharat stood firm on their professional commitments. They worked hard and lined-up several blue-chip investor interactions. It was going to be their last assignment at CSLA, and they wanted to close their innings in style, on a hugely successful note.

On many investor interaction meetings, we ran into DLF's management team, which was also there to make an investment pitch. DLF's investor interaction team comprised of 5-7 people gravely contrasted our team composition, which on most occasions had only one of us along with a CLSA representative. We were massively outnumbered on headcount.

However, CLSA's splendid marketing efforts ensured that we got our share of time from senior analysts and relevant fund managers.

The final results of our intense, three week's global road-show with over 75 investor meetings was quite rewarding. We had set ourselves a target to raise $240 million, and we generated around a 2.3-time subscription. We build a book of close to $550 million, by the time we closed.

It was a phenomenal result. Though we ended up restricting the issue size to our required capital amount, it was indeed gratifying to successfully conclude a highly intense exercise, which had a fair share of drama, excitement, challenges and learning.

For me, I learnt the importance of trust and faith. The Board trusted Ananth, who believed me in my judgment on appointing the sole merchant banker. In spite of some mid-course turbulence, Analjit and Ananth's confidence did not waver. This demonstration of trust pushed the team's resolve to succeed. It was a natural outcome of backing the team.

We trusted CLSA for their track record and capabilities. CLSA's professionalism, including the commitment demonstrated by their exiting executives, was an eye-opener. Once we reposed faith and trust on them, there was no looking back.

My key learning from this experience with CLSA was — the organisation stands taller than any individual. If the organisation is system and processes oriented, in the short-term, it has the capacity and capability to overcome any challenge.

Lastly, the merits of placing a high-quality investment opportunity before sophisticated investors ensured we could garner resources even with a potential conflict with DLF's fundraising. The underlying quality of our businesses and the potential for long-term value creation were definitely attractive propositions for the investors. It was duly reflected in their subscription of our offer.

Chest Out, Shoulders Back, Chin Up

Arvind Passey

Do I intend taking you on a walk-through of the Indian Military Academy? No.

There won't be any OG-clad soldiers sprinting by the side of words in this post.

There won't be any shorts-clad RSS sevaks waiting to guide you into some disciplinary mumbo jumbo unique to them.

We shall go for a short walk into the heart of the discipline, allowing it complete freedom to express whatever it wishes to and in any way.

What better place to start than the kitchen of my home where we have every sort of masala and other ingredients that may be used to whip, chip, grill or drill a great meal. Each container here has a label that is always looking straight into your eyes. By the way, even the cosmetics kept on the dresser follow this discipline and so does the stuff kept in the small shelf in the bathroom that alternates as a store for our toiletries. Even the books in the study, the clothes on our hangers, the hangers themselves, the clothes out on the balcony and drying follow a pattern and must face the same direction.

In fact, everywhere in our home is a silent reminder of the command grilled into my being:

'Chest out – Shoulders back – Chin up'.

Try this command on yourself for a start. Repeating 'Chest out – Shoulders back – Chin up' will invariably find anyone looking for a new person. Someone is looking straight ahead and right into the eyes of anyone who is standing in front, and you are this someone. You'll like it. You'll love it… and there is no reason why containers, hangers, books, and other objects within the home should not feel proud of a bit of regimentation in their lives.

Twenty-eight years back when I got married, this was among the first segments of regimentation placed before my wife. Specky, my wife, nodded, smiled, and said, 'No wonder we're together. I'm so like you.'

I said, 'I learnt this while at the Indian Military Academy. My instructor did say that this will not be something easily forgotten, misplaced, or misinterpreted.'

'Well,' said Specky, 'I have never been even remotely close to the army, but even I love walking straight… and living straight.' We smiled and knew we were indeed made for each other.

Let me tell you a secret before I cleared my CDSE and joined the IMA; I was a grand slob. I took pride in calling my room 'the universe of chaos', and my mother was quite fed up with cleaning my room. I remember telling her once that my room was representative of discipline in chaos. 'Really?' asked mother.

I looked into her eyes and replied, 'I can search for anything I want, in record time.' But I knew this wasn't the complete truth as I had to sweat it out every time anything was needed. So searching for a book or a photocopied certificate or a sharpened pencil, or even that naughty bottle of black ink gave way to these skirmishes with time and urgency. Books continued having their spine facing away from me. Pencils were invariably thrust with force with the pointed end down. Photocopied documents were never in the right file… and ink bottles somehow always managed to practice evasive tactics. By the way, this does not mean that other rooms not in my charge were any better. The kitchen, for instance, was the place where I could never find anything on time and always had to shout for my mother, 'Mummy, which container has sugar?'

And then my mother would shout back her instructions from the bedroom, 'The first shelf has all the ingredients you need to make tea.' It was never, 'Pick the third container from the left on the second shelf from the top.' So I had to open the containers and find out the ones that had tea leaves and sugar. There was no discipline in our kitchen then. Every bottle, every container 'slouched' and went on with their lives in a rather disorganised way!

But all this changed in the first week at the Academy.

We were taught that every label needed to face the user and that everything had a specific position on the table. It was all new to me.

I mumbled, 'This is ridiculous. Why must the toothpaste be kept first and then the shaving cream tube? Why must they always be on the left side of the dresser top? Why must they be placed in a way to make their name obvious and readable?'

One of my seniors then gently informed me that this was because even if I got up in the dead of night and there was no electricity, I'd pick up my toothbrush without disturbing anything else and be able to squeeze out toothpaste and not my shaving cream on it even with my eyes closed! Believe it or not, I did all this after spending a fortnight barely in the Academy. I was asked to enter each cabin there in the platoon quarters and see for myself how things were laid out. I saw, and I learnt.

I asked, 'But why do we call this a Chest out – Shoulders back – Chin up sequence here sir?'

'Because this is what you are going to learn to do in life. And if you do it, you'll be a good soldier and never store bullets in the wrong pouch. TIt his is the way we live to fight another battle. And, by the way, every object, even the inanimate ones, need to do it so as not to disturb the fabric of discipline anywhere.' The last part confused me, but I was happy to have understood the value of the rest of his short lecture.

These little laws, I reckoned, could make even housework so much easier. Ah! I know there is no escape from housework.

Housework? The word takes me back to another snippet from my own life where I was made to understand the difference between housework and homework... the latter gets you a pat from the boss at home, but the former is vital for the dreams on which generations are nurtured.

What? How can homework be so important?

Let me recount another story from my days in the OGs. One of my instructors at the Indian Military Academy was rather fond of repeating 'the more you sweat in training, the less you bleed in war'. So, one day I collected my courage, marched up to him and asked, 'What is the importance of 'more' in what you're saying, sir?'

'An intelligent question… like all questions asked by GCs of course… 'more' is simply reminding you to do your homework.'

I can tell you I couldn't have been more intrigued. One word that I was unable to decipher then had led to another that made the entire quote sound like a thriller where the cues were well hidden. Nevertheless, the instructor explained, we need to go beyond our brief, beyond what was happening during the official training time and continue conditioning of our body and mind even during our free hours. That, he said, is homework. 'And no officer can hope to become a good officer without concentrating on his homework,' he concluded, before leaving us to march off in squads to the next class.

Years later, I now realise how important homework is. It is like the extensive research I do before I sit down to write even a short blog post. It was the reading I always did before I met a team of media planners from some newspaper to negotiate a deal for my organisation when I was heading Corporate Communications. It was akin to all the interactions and orientations the salesman within me needed before I went out in the market to sell a product. Homework is what enables dreams to survive. It is almost like a parent restructuring his knowledge and information in anticipation of all that his child will need from him years later. Yes, homework is also a bridge that connects a parent to a kid.

Kids need their parents to do a lot of homework. He (or she) looks at the world and starts dreaming of the way he is going to contribute as an adult… He may wish to become a writer, an actor, an architect, an explorer, or even an entrepreneur of a start-up. After all, the kids today have more access to information than the earlier generations ever had. However, to even get closer to those dreams, the kid would need his parent to converse with obstacles and help him overcome them. These barriers could be about help in sourcing information to getting access to the right amount of funding. Knowing about these obstacles, understanding them, finding and adopting the ways to get over them are all a part of the homework for a parent. It is all about knowing how to plan for a child's future. It was what my instructor at the academy was talking about.

Homework for adults isn't a joke. Well, it isn't something to make you knit your brows and think of terrible things happening if you fumble while doing it. I believe that every small effort to recognise the importance of homework is what finally gets it done… done well, if I may add. Life is all about believing in the Chest out – Shoulders back – Chin up logic that I was taught the tough way.

But then life isn't always about keeping the toothpaste back, where it is to be kept and understanding the difference between housework and homework… another facet that I have keenly tried to influence my family and friends with is about managing time well.

Let me go back in time and try to remember an incident that is again from my days spent at the Indian Military Academy.

This happened sometime in the late seventies and is fondly remembered by everyone around me at home. I have nicknamed this incident 'The watch that refused to tell the truth'.

'I'm sorry I'm late. I forgot to look at my watch!' No, I did not tell this to the Battalion Commander.

I went a step further, and when he pointed out that I was a good half-hour late in reaching, I replied, 'My watch says I'm on time, sir.'

My watch indeed reflected what I said, but not because it was 1530 hours, but because I had made it to lie.

I knew I had to be in the minor OT (Obstacles training) ground for my remaining BPETs (Battle Proficiency and Endurance Tests) at sharp 1530 hours, but we had an 'outdoors' class that day, and it was already 3 by the time I reached the mess.

'No, I'm not going to miss my lunch,' I thought and smiled at the next thought, 'Let the Colonel wait.' A small voice within me egged me on to finish my lunch fast, change into my dungarees, get my rifle issued from the kot (a place where weapons are kept) and reach the spot for the test, but I chose not to listen to it.

As I unhurriedly strolled back to my cabin in the Company Lines, the CSM (Company Sargent Major) saw me and said in a horrified voice, 'The BO is waiting for you. He has sent a message asking you to be there 'on the double'. The Military Academy is a place where everything happens 'on the double'... which, in simple language just meant, I had to sprint into my dungarees, sprint over to the kot and sprint to the OT area.

'GC 15124 reporting, sir.'

'You're late. What happened?'

'My watch says I'm on time, sir.'

He bent to peer into my watch and then gave me an incredulous look, 'OK. Let's see if you clear the 9 ft ditch, the monkey-rope, and the fireman lift today one after the other.'

It does not matter what happened after this.

It does not matter that I flunked my BPETs.

All that matters is what the Battalion Officer said as he left, 'Watch your watch carefully, or you'll fail to get anywhere.'

Now, every time my maid skips a workday and comes with her reason... or when my designer in the office a few years back wanted to get around some scheduled task for the sake of his work... or when my son, who is now an architect and in London, wanted to lean on some excuse for not wanting to do his assignment... every time I see someone look for an excuse for not working or avoiding, I say, 'Watch your watch carefully, or you'll fail to get anywhere.'

Stories stick to the mind, and they have a good reason to do this. Nevertheless, stories happen because they somehow want you to carry them and maybe share them in many ways with multiple people at different times.

A Strange Introduction

Prabhakar Mundkur

'Hari Om' says a calm, quiet voice as the door opens. I am surprised to see a fair-skinned woman of average height dressed in ochre robes. She is barefooted. 'Hari Om' I say very self-consciously. The words are not strange, but I have to admit I have never wished anyone like that in a long time. Thoughts race through my mind. Why have I come here? Did I do the right thing? Who is this foreigner who is using our spiritual language to greet me? Somehow I resent it. Is it one of those ashrams that foreigners have taken charge of in India? I somehow had always hated the thought of foreigners adopting our spirituality and then dishing it back to us neatly labelled and packaged. Spirituality in a toothpaste tube. Press, and it will ooze out. Press harder, and more of it will ooze out.

Come in, she says very quietly. My mind quickly comes back to the present. She leads me to a table and chair. The room is bare, just like whatever I can see of the rest of the house. This is Khira Nagar in Santacruz West. I quickly think this place obviously functions like some ashram, as I spy on another woman in ochre robe's rustling through the flat.

'Yes, how can I help you?' says the quiet voice behind the ochre robe as I sit uncomfortably on the edge of my chair. She introduces herself as Swami Nityamuktananda. 'Swami? Nityamuktananda? Who may have named her that I think? Why do these foreigners come to Mumbai and take on these Indian names and call themselves Swami? Am I getting put off? Relax, I say to myself. This is the last resort. You have to be patient, says a voice inside of me.'

'Roshan Mundkur' sent me here I say a little reluctantly. 'Wish Roshan had told me they were foreigners. I might have given it a second thought and checked that well-known yoga school on the eastern side of Santacruz'. 'She said you could help me' I continue. 'What is the problem' she says quietly. 'Why is she asking me what is the problem? Do people come here only if they have a problem? I begin to realise that this is a yoga school being run quietly out of Khira Nagar by the 3 female monks. What is the problem? Yes, I need to tell her what the problem is. Should I come clean? My first response is "There is no problem, really" I say. She waits patiently for me to continue, with an understanding look.'

'But recently, I have been having some problems with my breathing'. The words almost stumble out of my mouth. 'What kind of breathing problems' she says quietly. Should I just blurt out the truth? This is my chance. I have been diagnosed with asthma I say. 'No problem' she says. No problem? I don't think she quite understands the trauma I have gone through. The deriphyllin injections that I had to take to make my way to Ulka every day; the cortisone tablets; the feeling of getting choked; Near-death; almost an injection a day, and then when the injections stopped, it would be Ok for another 2 weeks, and the problem would recur, and the ayurvedic doc from Chembur who duped me. How would one know that an innocent looking herbal powder, the colour of coffee that worked miraculously on me would be packed with cortisone?

'It will go' she says confidently. I suddenly feel comforted. No one has said these words to me before. Hope. 'How long will it take?' I ask expectantly? 'You should feel better in 6 months' she says. Relief. 'These things are all psychosomatic' she says. Psychosomatic? This is 1982. And the word hasn't entered our vocabulary as an everyday language yet. What is she saying? Is something wrong with me? Is she actually accusing me of being psycho-something? Is she saying something is mentally wrong with me? My God. I wish I didn't come here to hear this. She interrupts my thoughts with 'It is normal'. Oh, so being psycho is the new normal. Jesus Christ, what is all this?

Our conversation is over. I leave, and she sees me off at the door with a smile. I am to see her next Monday for my first class. How should I address her, I wonder? She says 'Hari Om'. ' Hari Om Swamiji'. I stumble on 'swamiji'. Why should I call some foreigner dressed as a monk in ochre robes a Swamiji?

A Journey into the Unknown

Many months later, I am already feeling better. My God, Swamiji Nityamuktananda has exorcised the devil of asthma out of my body. I am doing well at work. I don't quite know how to thank Roshan Mundkur. Roshan is the wife of Bal Mundkur, who is a distant uncle, or distant cousin. I am not quite sure because our families are quite close. His mother Kripabaiakka is always in and out of my house, quite often spending her weekends with us.

One day, I am doing Surya-Namaskar at the ashram with my eyes closed, saying the mantra, focusing on my breath, being aware of a different chakra with every posture of the namaskar. Suddenly, I hear her say 'Do it dynamically'. Dynamically? Wonder what that means? Fast? Quick? Forceful? My mind races to find out the meaning of 'dynamically'. I flex my muscles. I am doing each pose in the namaskar more quickly. I am using my strength while going down to the floor. Suddenly, I hear the words 'STOP'. 'Lie down' she says. I catch my breath. 'Relax' she says. 'Let all the tension leave your body'. 'Slowly'

A few minutes later, she asks me a question, a question that throws me off balance. 'Are you in a very stressful job?' She says. Stressful? Stupid Advertising. Of course, it is stressful. You miss a deadline, and you have hell to pay. You work late into the night because clients make unreasonable demands. Why do I always have to work hard because the marketing director is travelling next week? So he wants to see everything this week? Why? Is he going to give us a decision this week? No. He is going to travel, and when he gets back, he is going to take his own sweet time to tell us what he thinks of it. So why the hell does he want to see it this week? I have a good mind to tell that stupid manager, that it is impossible. Screw them. Yes, that's precisely what I am going to do. Bal Mundkur taught us to be brave. So what am I doing getting pulverised by a nit-wit of a brand manager? I must not weaken just because I am young, married and already have a daughter. If I lose my job, I am sure I am bright enough to still look after my family.

Suddenly, I am brought to the present from my half-conscious state of doing yoga-nidra. Yoga-Nidra is like a trip. It sometimes reminds me of my LSD trips. The only difference is that I can snap back to the present reality when I want to. So my mind is still within my control, unlike with acid.

'Yes Swamiji', I respond. 'Which profession' she asks? 'I am in advertising', I say hesitantly. No response. Is there a quiet disdain that I can't hear? Wonder what she is thinking. I can't tell with my eyes closed. I think it is time to break the silence. 'Why?' I ask.

And then she replies 'Because you have got used to the idea that dynamism means tension' she says. I have to think about this carefully. My intellectual mind is 100% alert now. What? Dynamism and tension? What made her say that? 'Why do you say that Swamiji' I say. 'Because when I asked you to do the Surya Namaskar dynamically, you got all tensed up. You started using your strength. You used the pressure from your muscles.' 'So how do I do it?' I ask quickly. The only answer I get is 'You will understand, one day'.

That simple exposition on a word that I thought I knew so well disturbed me for the next many months. The dictionary definition of dynamism is 'a process or mechanism responsible for the development or motion of a system'. Yes, that definition did not have force or energy. Some other definitions did. How do I figure out what she really meant? And what is the meaning of I will understand one day. Which day. When? Why not now? All these questions raced through my mind.

Many months later, Swami Satyananda Saraswati of the Bihar School of Yoga accidentally steps on my feet while walking in a crowded area. Immediately Swami Nityamuktananda asks me 'Swamiji stepped over you. Are you hurt?' And then she laughs her characteristic laugh. 'No, in fact, it was as if a feather walked over me.' I tell her. Immediately she asks 'Do you think Swamiji is dynamic?' 'Very.' I reply. 'Do you think his dynamism is associated with force and strength?' she says. I must admit that Swami Satayanand is dynamic without using force and energy. Is she trying for me to get the meaning of dynamism a few months later after I first got rattled by the concept? Later in the evening in the Ashram at Munger, Swami Niranjananada speaks for about 15 minutes on yoga and philosophy. The amazing thing is that after he finishes his speech in English, he immediately speaks the same content in Spanish and Italian. I am amazed and enthralled at the end of the 45 minutes. I say to Swami Nityamuktananda, 'What a dynamic speaker. I was floored'. And she says 'And did you think the dynamism had force and strength in it?' I have to admit that surprisingly it didn't. In fact, he never moved during the 45 minutes. He never waved his arms animatedly while speaking. I can swear that his arms were neatly tucked away under his robe, and they stayed there till the end of his speech. Were there any animated facial expressions? No. Did he move even once No. Was he still dynamic? Yes.

Life's Lessons passed on to Professional Life.

It is 8 years later. I have been told there is nothing more for me to learn after being inducted into some higher, secret yogas. I am back in Mumbai. I have to make a very important presentation to S M Datta, Chairman of the then Hindustan Lever. Lever's has asked their agencies to study one competitor each. Presentations are to be made to the Chairman and the Board. I have selected P & G. My presentation is called 'Know the Enemy'. These are days before the Internet in 1991. Before Sun Tzu was to get quoted by everybody. I have decided this is the presentation of my life. Everyone is nervous. Mike Khanna, always a picture of poise, is biting his nails. Anil Bhatia is making jokes nervously trying to diffuse the tension. I start the presentation. 'Dynamism without tension' are the only words in my mind. No unnecessary body movement. Hand movements or other gestures. No facial contortions to make a point. A point can be made without all this. Control your breathing. It has to be even. It has to be relaxed. It is one of the most tedious 60 minutes of my life in the Hindustan Lever Boardroom. I finish with a quote from Sun Tzu. 'If you know the enemy…'. There is thundering applause.

We walk down the flights of Lever House and wait for Mike's car in the foyer at Lever House, Backbay Reclamation. Suddenly, Mike extends his hand. 'You made me proud to belong to Thompsons today.' he says.

It's time for a celebration.

Sunshine Is Always On The Other Side Of The Storm

Arvind Passey

Storms aren't to be feared. When you emerge from one, you are a different person… you have probably reinvented, restructured, and reactivated elements that have the potential of changing the direction of more than one facet connected with your life. I mean your professional life. Yes, this works even on the personal plane. There will always be a difference between words that tell and incidents that show… and there are a few who remind me of the times I dared to enter a storm… or a stormy debate when I was heading corporate communications.

'One designer?' I asked, with disbelief written all over, 'Just one designer to assist me in getting all the artworks done?'

BBB, as he was addressed, the head of the largest financial company in India that had excelled in arbitraging in the obfuscating but energising world of stocks and shares, was known to be a man who tried to get more things done with less workforce. He looked at me and smiled, 'You need to teach the designer to do more in less time. That's it.'

I tried explaining to him that times had changed a lot from getting approvals for every artwork by moving files with half-baked ideas in a print format. Files waiting for a nod after the other vital meetings to get over were no longer the norm and that every blink was going to be expense-intensive. Moreover, the expertise of designers who were comfortable with CorelDraw and Photoshop simply had to be augmented with a more than working knowledge of Indesign and Flash. The artworks were no longer for massive outdoor, pamphlets, paper inserts, and print advertisements… there was the surreal world of animated banners for websites, landing pages, and e-mailers slowly making their impact felt in businesses. The customers, which included a lot of potential students in the finance courses that the company had interests in, were all net-savvy and wanted informative variety faster than one designer could ever dream of doing.

The CEO blinked and murmured, 'Is the world really going this way?'

I looked at him perplexed and answered, 'Yes, and there is more to it all. Online analytics is becoming vital and knowing the profiles of people who bumble on to our pages is important. This gives us an edge over the competitors. Google Adsense is not something that can be done without an expert tinkering away for long hours. Even beyond office hours.'

The small outburst seemed to have some effect, but I could see that the tussle wasn't yet over.

I decided to educate him about the complex scientific meanderings that needed to graduate to become an art-form in deciding the keywords that needed to be a part of the complete online package. 'And so sir,' I went on, 'it isn't just another designer who has a knack for understanding what clicks and what survives and gets followed in the fast-moving universe of the online impact that we need. We need people who have been to the depths and know what is right and appropriate.'

The little game of soliciting customers to reach out and add the profit margins was no longer limited to buying contact lists from unscrupulous vendors for small change and then depending on the hordes of tele-callers who thought they were masters in teleselling. The consumer was becoming far more intuitively intelligent and wanted endorsements from every sort of medium which was accessible.

Let me add here that all this happened around ten years ago and those were times when not every business had taken a firm decision on the facets that I was talking about. The marketing teams from the dailies and the magazines and periodicals too were subtle enough not to let their counterparts from the online portals get even a whiff of what the under-currents were like.

Fortunately for me, the CEO decided to let his son enter the dynamic world of this new-age decision-making, and this is probably one of the factors that saved the day for us. He was convinced of all that I had in mind even before I could voice my concerns and said, 'Just wait. Let me see if I can convince my father.'

When you are working in an organisation that is managed at the top by a family, one can and must try to see if there is anyone who will connect to the thought-processes that were too challenging for the older generation to grasp. We were now a team of two, and I did end up having a team of two designers and was supplemented by one person from the IT section to help us with online analytics.

Well, smaller companies do have a knack for discovering solutions that do not seem to offset the perceived added costing and did try to rotate people in strange and unimaginable ways that make everyone happy. The designer whom we ultimately got was another employee who worked in another subsidiary and did the in-office artworks. He had just begun learning some of the applications that were desperately needed to get us going. What is important here is that one needs to put one's foot down firmly and ask for talents instead of being made to look like an idiot for being unable to match the speed at which the communications industry decided to move.

Another incident when I had to fight a seemingly lost battle was in the company that I worked for before joining this financial juggernaut. This company was headquartered in Indore because the CEO projected himself as one whose dreams began in a garage. This garage syndrome had been picked up even by the audio-visual media, and he was never tired of telling me his stories of how he managed his start-up single-handed for the first few months. 'Yes, growth means that we had to invite other people too,' he said, 'and build all the systems painstakingly.'

The registered office was in Indore, and they had the foresight to have a corporate office in Delhi. I was one of the first staffers and was heading corporate communications from Delhi... but I was constantly badgered to spend more and more time with him in Indore. This flying back and forth from Delhi to Indore was not just exhausting but appeared meaningless.

'I think you need to spend more time in Indore,' said SM, as he always insisted on being addressed as. He was the CEO of this company that had then more around forty centres spread all over India. Centres of excellence, as he always insisted on adding, because after all, many of the entrants in the IIMs went through this academy. In the coming two years we did manage to more than double this count, and the impact. The following of this coaching institute was immense.

It will be interesting here to tell you of the way I was managing communications strategies from Delhi with my team sitting in Indore. I know this sounds far-fetched, but we, fortunately, had complete and fast access to the Internet as well as mobile communication to pull our victories without hiccups. So from ideation to research and then on to the initial drafts of all sorts of artworks was done by us sitting hundreds of miles away from each other.

My presence was essential in Delhi as the bulk of the media planning was done from here, which included too many interactions with marketing teams from the worthy to all the media trash that existed. After all, a pan-India impact was simply impossible by pursuing the local media at Indore. Dainik Bhaskar, Jagran, and Amar Ujala were not the only papers that could contribute to this dream... and other publications always found it difficult to conduct their negotiations with a client who wanted them to travel repeatedly to his favourite city. There were then the day-to-day issues of intense follow-ups for page positioning, add-ons, and awareness about every new media innovation that was breaking out of its shell.

There was hardly any incentive for me to spend an unrealistic time away from Delhi, and so I told the CEO, 'I think my visits to Indore need to be curtailed. There is a lot happening at Delhi, and every day of absence means we have a high probability of missing out on a new way we could use to get the right public perception.' What I also mentioned was that the PR agency we had hired at a ridiculously low rate of retainer-ship needed continual guidance. You will be surprised at the kind of media exposure I could get just because I was always after them to go beyond a mere mention in a generic article in print or a presence on a portal that our target group was hardly interested in. The online blitz too had started, and we did not want to miss any of this fun as well. Fortunately, the CEO was perceptive enough to realise how vital all this online presence was and was slowly inching towards a better budgetary allocation to this segment as compared to the more expensive print media and the hilariously cost-intensive av-media.

When no amount of good-natured reasoning seemed to be working, I decided to change my tactics. I soon realised that my being a good speaker had a lot to do with it. He loved handing me the task of anchoring all the big and small PR events that were in Indore. Yes, Indore was their fortress, and they could not be seen as losing out to any of the other players who were proactive there... But listen, all this was being done at the expense of what a good communications team could manage from the Capital.

All I was doing during my stays at Indore was anchoring events, writing just-in-time scripts for the CEO's many speeches, and monitoring the way the hands of the designers glided over the keyboard. These designers anyway never liked being goaded by me like this.

It wasn't doing me any good and seemed like a monstrous black-hole sucking me in. I had to think of a way out. An escape plan was what I needed. A plan to help me go back to Delhi where I was required… And, at the same time, gave the Indore office the sort of talent they were starving for.

There was enough time at my disposal in Indore, and I decided to convince the brighter among the faculty that they needed to think beyond just going to their class and rattling-off all the solutions to the complexities in math and language. 'A better life waits for you,' I told them, 'if you increase your skills levels.'

So I convinced the CEO for small two-hour communication workshops daily where I would train them to take over tasks like anchoring events and writing incisive articles that could even be sent to me for getting published in newspapers wherever we had space bought for such efforts. In less than three months, my team of effective communicators was ready… and let me add that this was possible because I was handling communication sessions for the centre directors who were called in batches every month. I was accustomed to telling them all about our current communication strategies, introduce the annual plan for advertising and PR, and even hold informative sessions on how to edit artworks and manage a few tasks at their end.

The storm that I was often creating about wanting to go back to Delhi was finally controlled, and I could see the sun shining through the dark ominous clouds as the CEO said, 'So you have managed to wriggle out of staying in Indore. However, I will keep calling you every time I feel it is necessary.'

'I shall be there whenever you need me, Sir.' I knew I had gained more than just a longer stay in Delhi... I was now more comfortable training others, and 'there will be so much more text to edit and make it print-worthy,' I murmured as I sat in the cab that sped away to the airport.

Storming the storm is an idea not to be feared. All that is needed is an unflinching resolve to march ahead on a concept once convinced. Effective management is all about this resolve as sunshine is waiting patiently on the other side of the storm.

The Calling

Tanya Kotnala

'You know you should probably do away with the belt, such an eyesore!'

'Really?' I spent the whole afternoon drafting its pattern! Now, it's a waste!

Komal, lost in the search for her bobbin case, with a hasty smile, handed me over a strip of disprins .

'Thank you' I tore open two tablets and watched them dissolve in a plastic mineral water bottle. The radial pattern looked soothing. I wiped the dew off the skylight, right next to my industrial stitching machine, took a deep breath and stared into nothingness. I haven't slept for almost 5 days now; it was a week before placements, and the final graduation fashion show was just a few weeks away.

'Don't you think you're too ambitious with the whole thing, I mean you need to prepare your portfolio for the placements.'

'Not applying at the placements and it's final!.' I abruptly snatched my hand embroidered fabric from Vishal, who was still checking out my techniques.

Not that I wanted to hide any masterwork from him, I didn't want him to point out any blunders now! I designed well but couldn't stitch cleanly; good tailoring requires several calculations, fabric understanding, loads of focus; to be honest, it's plain god gifted. I was already having a hard day! Plus Vishal could get into details and often on one's nerves.

'You know, Prof says that you and Komal have the brightest chances at the placements, think over it' Vishal's voice faded in the milieu as I scurried far past him to focus on the undone belt.

Late at night as soon as my upper lip kissed the black coffee filled mug, the lower retreated concluding that it was too hot to drink, I looked at my unfinished garments and said to myself 'Vishal is right, it's just too ambitious!

But then, it's not my style to do something customary; a collection should be inspiring, people must look at it and feel enchanted, not only by the aesthetics of it but also the innovative techniques drawn in. Still not sure whether it was worth skipping the placements, but the condition of my collection was critical; I could end up flunking the semester because of unfinished garments, I was left with no choice.

Connecting the dots of my life so far, I knew I don't have what it takes to be a well settled, organised and financially well off person, reason? I blame it on my artistic soul, from garments to life, people often tell me that I am too ambitious and impractical. I had learnt my lesson due to my past miscalculations.

I would constantly desire to bring innovation to design. I planned well, designed fine but had the most laid back execution strategy. The past projects that looked ground-breaking on blueprint copies turned out to be shabby when manufactured; I was never satisfied with the finished outcome, always felt that it needed additional time and efforts. I had to turn things around this time and keep my approach minimal and universal. Turn down the volume of my over pushy artistic soul and try being mature.

But even after planning strategically and executing efficiently, my collection seemed impossible to walk the ramp. My stitches were haywire, my fitting wasn't very appealing and let's not discuss my psychological well being back then.

The jury day found me extremely panicky. I worked until the very end moment, the overall finish of the garment wasn't up to the mark. I was mentally prepared to be roasted by the jury members.

While standing outside the Jury room waiting for my turn, I could feel my feet shaking and realised that the more you focus, the shakier they get. One of the models handed me a glass of water and asked me to calm down; the very next second my name was called out. I stood in front of the fashion industry's most experienced designers; I felt naked!

I handed over my research and mood boards and started talking; surprisingly, I sounded confident!

'The problem is you should know when to stop!' 'The jury member continued 'I think you got so excited about the technique part that you went too far with it; you should know when to stop'.

Exposed in less than 30 seconds.

'The blend of techniques is very unique, good research work, you have used extremely challenging fabrics. I like your guts.' said another Jury member. All the seven members nodded in agreement.

'You have a lot of things going on, but they all are stylish and ready.' said another member. My jury went on for about half an hour; they analysed everything from fabrics to finishing. As soon as I stepped out of the room, it was too vague for me to decide whether it went well or was I doomed?

'I like your guts.' echoed in my head 'I like your guts.' I muttered to myself.

Soon the Graduation Fashion show concluded, and to my surprise, I won two golds and the best craft project trophy.

'I am to join in a week.' I felt Komal's soft pat over my shoulder. I suddenly realised that I was the only student in my batch with no job! 'Already? That's great news! 'I replied with a dim smile.

What followed can be described as a month of confusion. Some of my family associates fixed up a few job interviews for me. I would get through the most, but something or the other would turn disagreeable.

I was disappointed with myself. At a young, restless age, when my peers were joining their desired jobs, aiming sky high, getting ready to work and gaining experience, I was still there at square one, with no excitement about industry jobs. After sessions of introspection, I decided to do, what unsure people usually end up doing; I decided to pursue studies.

One day, out of the blue, my mentor from the institute called. She was excited to share that based on my graduation craft fashion project; the institute would want me to consider an opportunity to work with the Sikkim weavers under a project by the Ministry of Textiles.

A few days later I received a life-changing call from the Ministry confirming the Sikkim project allotment.

'Yes, I'll do it! Didn't even let the officer finish clearing up the brief.

The project was more of a voluntary type, and you would be right to see it as a workshop conducted for a few months. A project was aiming at local craft product development, innovation, uplift and women empowerment. However, for me, it was an excellent opportunity to explore the beautiful scenic Sikkim!

I was already dreaming of orchids, Snow lion dances, the Kanchenjunga. I was in my Dimsum heaven!

Instead, I got posted at Melli Bazaar.

Melli is a diminutive town located at the borders of Sikkim, Siliguri. (West Bengal) It is right across a bridge (over the mighty Teesta). Forget about snow lions; the temperature was like you could poach an egg right in the open. It was plain dark, ghostly and sticky hot (humid) would be a better description of the hell I was walking in.

The motel overcharged for noisy geckos, saturated walls and damp blankets. Dinner was heaps of half boiled rice served with watery dal and some turmeric coated -oil dripping French fries.

All this at rupees eight hundred and fifty for a night 'God what have I gotten into?'

My wakeup call the next morning was not the rainfall music on my mobile but the noise of excited screaming geckos making love. Sweating out of terror I rolled, mummified in a damp bed sheet and ran towards the first exit I saw, and I barged open what I thought was the door!

I found myself standing in the small cosy balcony, facing one of the most amazing views! I could smell the mighty Teesta's clear water and almost feel the fragrance filled hydrangeas! Or was it the other way round? I don't remember thinking at all! I was so stunned!

The 4-month project went pretty well. I was applauded for my work and management at the centre. We had finished 20 beautiful handcrafted products. And I had one hell of an experience.

On the eve of my departure from Sikkim, one of the dearest friends called, just to inquire about my whereabouts. We ended up discussing a lot of things that day, but let me share the tiny but most relevant part of the discussion with you.

'I read your updates about the Sikkim trip on FB, see you doing great things, and it's just the beginning for you. Do you still feel the same way about being successful? He chuckled.

'How can you define success? I don't even know if such a thing exists. You must just appreciate the beauty of now, keep doing things that I love and eventually, I believe everything will fall into place!

'So when are you joining the industry?' 'Never! I am too child- like minded for that.'

We discussed quite a few things that day, and my spirit had finally answered me. Suddenly, I knew where I was headed.

Wherever my instinct led me to. 'Listen to your heart; it knows what it wants.'

I am 23 now, have worked for a couple of rural ministry projects, freelanced for a few start-ups, and now the wavelengths of my heart have changed their meter. I am impatient but confident that it's time to launch my brand. Life is never what you expect it to be. Just erase all the expectations and start doodling your own experiences.

Thank You

Raman Kalia

Since a very young age, we are told by our parents, teachers, movies, and society about doing the right thing.

But what is the right thing?

Is it about sacrificing?

Is it about not wanting the good things? Is it only about giving?

Does the right thing mean a life of hardship without pleasures? Is it about giving away the fun things?

When I was young, about 8 or 9 years old, we were staying in a huge British time bungalow in Faridkot. My father was part of the Punjab Civil Services, which meant that we used to change cities, homes, schools, and even friends every few years. Faridkot is a district in the state of Punjab. It is named after Baba Farid, a Sufi Saint and a Muslim missionary.

The Faridkot I am referring to was still a part of Ferozepur district. The house we stayed in was opposite to a railway station. Speaking of which, the never-ending sounds of trains chugging and hooting at all hours built my life-long fascination for the trains. Strangely even today, whenever I change my residences, there always is a railway line passing close to it. I don't know whether it is coincidence, or I subconsciously choose a rented apartment on this basis.

The house we lived in Faridkot was a circular one-story building, with more rooms than needed. The boundary walls were lined with trees of various varieties and to our delight a large garden to play in. My siblings and I played all kinds of games that make sense only at that age.

One day, my brother and I were playing in the garden, when we saw a parrot that was stuck in the bushes. We pushed the branches to help him come out. However, the parrot was unable to do so and appeared very scared. Finally, my brother reached inside, held the parrot gently and eased him out. By now, the bird was reasonably scared, and despite our amateurish handling, it cooperated with us to let us get him free without any unwarranted aggression or a peck on our hands. We thought our 'good Samaritan' role would end the moment we could bring the parrot out.

So we put the bird down. We were sure he would fly away. However, to our surprise, the parrot just sat there looking at us. We tried to coax him.

Here, I am assuming the parrot was a he. We anyway had no way of telling the gender.

We were at a loss and unsure of what to do next. The idea of rescuing him was to set him free. Nevertheless, if we left him behind in the condition he was, he was sure to fall prey to some hungry cat. There was no way we could leave him out to fend for himself.

Left with no option, we decided to adopt him and take him home.

We were very clear about one thing. And that was not keeping the bird in a cage, as we hoped that he might want to remember how to fly at some point in time.

However, there was a challenge.

We also had a pet dog. We were scared and worried. He might harm the bird. With a dog named Hiti, short for Hitler, I guess it was a fair assumption. It meant that both had to be kept apart, all the time. We marked out the territory for the parrot and the dog. We ensured there was no overlap or any unwarranted interactions between the two. When the parrot was inside the house, the dog was kept out, and when we took the parrot out to the garden, we would bring the dog inside the house.

There used to be some incessant barking, but it never perturbed the bird.

The parrot happily adjusted to the new environment. Hopping from room to room, eating the food that we offered, he made our lives delightful in the process. He would stay in our room during the night and be generally quiet.

We tried to make him speak as we had seen in the movies, but we never succeeded in our effort.

Everyone was happy. The arrangement was final. We safely assumed he would be with us forever.

As it is with every story, that was not to be.

Just after a week, one day we were sitting in the garden, when my father picked up the parrot and put him on his forearm and said, 'This is how Maharajah Ranjit Singh used to keep his hawk.' The parrot stayed there for a second and then suddenly, he flapped his wings and flew away.

We looked at him in his flight, completely taken by surprise. We kept watching and thinking he would come back out of bonding, or get tired and return. However, soon, he was out of sight.

Was it the end of our friendship?

He was a joy when he stayed with us, and we felt sad when he flew away.

Then again, we always wanted him to fly. It was a mixed feeling of joy and sadness.

This logically should have been the end of our story. However, even that was not to be.

After three days, I heard my sister screaming and shouting for all of us. We ran outside and were greeted by an unbelievably beautiful sight. There were tens of parrots flying atop our house with one bird sitting down next to my sister. She was petting him, and he was quietly sitting by her side.

We knew that this was our parrot. He stayed with us for ten or fifteen minutes and met us all. We touched him and played with him. All this while, none of the other birds came down. They kept circling on top. After a while, he too flew away. This time, it was a final goodbye. And all of us just stood there smiling at each other. He never came back again but has stayed with us as a shared memory of the family.

This is not a narration about how nice we were, or whether we underestimate the intelligence of birds, or for that matter, how gratitude is always repaid. It is probably all of that. Nevertheless, none of it is the true significance. It is what I learnt, and I completely believe in it. It is all about doing the right thing not necessarily doing the thing right.

One of my professors once said that the branch that bears the fruit hangs low. Humility is not the absence of pride. It is the absence of haughtiness and abrasion.

We did not save the parrot so that we could have a pet or win his gratitude.

Businesses and brands need to have a similar outlook when it comes to dealing with the consumer. Profit cannot be a starting point for the work that you do. It should always be an outcome. The main motivation has to be a want to do good for the market and the consumer.

The existence of brands comes from their role to protect the consumer from the charlatans. It is about influencing the market for good. When you or your business or your brand enters the market, your presence should create a new world that is superior to the state in which you found it.

Unfortunately, what one finds in the brand behaviour and their approach is quite the contrary.

Brands have become charlatans. And the consumer needs protection from them now.

The market needs reshaping again. To overcome this new challenge, the market needs fresh solutions. But not necessarily new thinking. These solutions will come from the age-old thinking of doing the right thing. Doing good is not the right way to succeed. In my lessons of life, I have learnt that doing the right thing is the ONLY way to succeed.

The Storm

Farzana Suri

The world of an advertising agency is full of high drama; what with bizarre client deadlines, stressed Account Management teams and the equally harried Studio Managers. However, the fascinating part of these 'chaotic' moments are the office tales. You don't miss any theatrics of the soap operas aired on national TV if you happen to be a part of the agency tableau.

The tales stemming out of situations within the agency were innumerable. However, the most memorable ones to me were those related to clients, and they were in abundance.

One of them was truly special. It was at my stint with R K Swamy/BBDO in 2002 where I was managing the Italian brand, Piaggio's foray into commercial 3-wheelers. My strategic idea of penetrating the smaller cities through rural marketing had hit bull's eye, and I was made to lead the entire programme across the Southern states of India. It was exciting. And, one monsoon evening in July, I found myself heading to Udupi from Mumbai.

The Piaggio dealers were super enthused. An activity like a road-show was welcomed whole-heartedly by the sales team. I was to meet the most popular and successful dealer for Piaggio in Karnataka, S Padmanabhan. I had spoken to him several times earlier, and this was my first in-person meeting with him. He was already at the hotel to receive me, upon my arrival. He was tall, broad-shouldered and could have easily been in his late 50s. He was nattily dressed in a pristine white shirt and dark, well-tailored trousers that were carefully hemmed at the bottom and displayed signs of wear. His face had a light layer of face powder and was paler than his hands. He had the kindest, deep and moist pair of eyes. He was sporting a 90's Rajnikanth-esque hairstyle and stood out among the various guests in the hotel reception.

I smiled at him and said, 'Hello, Padmanabhan.' I continued, 'Rajni fan?' Rajnikanth is a Tamil superstar and an icon of the film industry. Padmanabhan beamed and in a deep voice responded reverently, 'Yes, Suri Ma'am!' 'Me, too!' I replied, gleefully. 'I saw Baba in Chennai, and I loved it! What's your favourite film?' He answered, animatedly 'Bassha, Ma'am. One of the best! Did you watch it?' and then peering at his watch, he stopped and said. 'Suri Ma'am, let's go to the showroom first. I want to introduce you to someone.' He hunched over as he spoke to me and led me towards the white Ambassador car waiting in the porch.

I liked this man!

The ride to his office was short, and the conversation was punctuated with Rajni tales in between discussions related to the road-show. As I stepped into the doorway of the showroom, my senses were assailed by spicy rasam, piping idlis and hmm… filter coffee.

'Wow! This smells and looks delicious!' I announced and heard my stomach growl in response. Padmanabhan delightedly replied, 'Suri Ma'am, my wife, Shobhana, has prepared it!' and I swear, I caught his chest widening a tad inch as he spoke. I looked up and saw his wife beaming in a crisp silk saree with a large vermillion dot on her forehead and the mangalsutra. She was standing next to the feast spread in my honour.

After gorging on the most delicious breakfast, I thanked Shobhana, and we both headed towards the town square where the road-show van awaited us. The loudspeaker blared Kannada songs, intermittently along with the brand, Ape's jingle. It was an incredibly windy day. I recall. Some of the people milling around the van were clutching at their mundus and saris. Rao, his Sales Manager, a young man in his 20s nodded at me and smiled, gesturing a 'namaste' as I waved a 'Hi!'

Padmanabhan and I waited on the far side of the van, in an attempt to shield ourselves from the strong gusts of wind. He stated, 'It looks like a storm, Suri Ma'am.' I just nodded. The banners flapped against the van, ripping themselves from the hooks. The wind enveloped all of us in the dust that brought along with it pieces of paper, dried leaves, plastic bags, thread, pieces of cloth and whatever seemed to lie comfortably on the ground. It also knocked off the standees near the van, ramming the shop signboards and causing them to swing hard.

A lady clutched her 5-year-old son who was almost blown away by the fury of the wind. Particles kept hurling at us from everywhere and, into every crevice and surface it could cloak. I kept clutching my hair, hating the mess it was creating. The dust had branded itself on every part of my clothing and body. And, I said to myself, 'What, in the blazes is going on? If this roadshow is a washout, the client won't pay!'

Padmanabhan, poor man held my elbow hard and ushered me into an alcove beside a store close by and where we both waited patiently for this sudden storm to quieten down. After what seemed like an eon, a calm settled around, albeit with a gentler breeze, and the onset of a welcoming drizzle. People began creeping out of their sanctuary, and everything started to inch towards normalcy.

I patted my clothes and hair, trying to dust off the mess, but it was pointless. My hair looked like it had been wrung vigorously in the washing machine without any detergent - I was as unclean as the storm could make me! I looked around to find Padmanabhan stroking his hair in place, in a desperate attempt to get all the foreign elements off his hair. I smiled and thought, 'He's as vain as me!'

I noticed some leaves on his shirt and dusted it off his back. My eyes then fell upon some thread-like strands that made their home in his hair. I said, 'Padmanabhan, there's something stuck in your hair.' Without waiting for a reply, I extended my hand and touched the back of his head. He was 5'9ish, and I went on my toes to dislodge the strands. I got hold of the strand. It was a sticky thread which had some particles of dust and hay-like things attached to it. It looked icky! I decided to pluck it out, gingerly. The icky threads kept clinging to more of his hair and refused to come off. I decided this needed more than just a gentle pull and tugged at it harder. 'This should make it come off', I thought. Just as I twisted to jerk it off, Padmanabhan turned his head around sharply and enquired with irritation, 'Has it come off?'

And, then we both froze!

I was clutching on to what looked like an entire head of hair that was dangling between my fingers! It looked like Rajnikanth's hair but with no head! I heard a voice scream at me, 'GIVE IT, BACK!!' My heart sank, and I was immobilised with shock and dread. My gaze followed the direction of the booming voice. It was Padmanabhan. His eyes no longer looked benign. They were imploring and struck with shame and embarrassment. I wished the earth would crack open, so I could cave into it. Silence rent the air despite the hum of the wind. I looked around and noticed the pairs of eyes and curving mouths of an audience watching this show!

It must have looked like a scene straight out of Mr Bean. I am clutching on to a hairpiece with wide eyes, bewildered and appalled. Padmanabhan, with his sparsely haired pate watching me in shock as if he was caught with his pants down. Shock and shame writ all over his face. Rao and three members of his team stopped in their tracks, their mouths perilously close to a guffaw!

At that very instant, Padmanabhan flailed his arms towards me and snatched the hairpiece and placed it back on his head, wearing it as best as he could. Our eyes met for a fleeting instant, and I was mortified! This could NOT be happening! Just then, Rao, hollered, 'Let's begin!' as he switched on the music. The road-show had begun, and it ended without any unforeseen event.

It was a quiet journey back to the hotel, that evening. Padmanabhan was silent while Rao kept chatting with the driver, now and then. The car pulled over at the hotel, and I bid goodbye.

Next morning, I received a call from Padmanabhan. He expressed his desire to drop by at the hotel before I left for the road-show in Mangalore, a city close to Udupi. I was uneasy. 'Why does he need to see me?' I asked myself. Honestly, I was extremely embarrassed over the incident and was uncomfortable facing him one-on-one. 'What the hell! Let's do it and get over it.' I told myself. The phone rang an hour later. Padmanabhan arrived and was waiting at the reception for me.

On reaching the lobby, I saw Shobhana, smiling and walking toward me but couldn't spot him. Shobhana was carrying a box of Mysore Pak, a special sweet, in a steel container with my name inscribed on it. She had made the sweets herself. I enquired about her husband, and she pointed toward a corner. I turned around. Padmanabhan was unrecognisable! He was in a white shirt with dark trousers – his pate gleaming with sparse grey hair under the bright lights of the lounge. He looked at me sheepishly, 'Suri Ma'am, I thought I'd take a leaf out of Thalaivar's book. When Thalaivar (Rajnikanth is referred as the leader) can be natural and loved for who he is, so can I, can't I?'

'Absolutely!' I nodded, vigorously in agreement with tears misting my eyes. Shobhana's eyes were moist as well;

love and pride were reflecting in them. This man had placed his vulnerability out there for everyone to see. I loved Padmanabhan, even more now. I gave him a tight hug.

While travelling back, I kept replaying the incident in my mind. And, the words of Haruki Murakami couldn't have rung more true, 'When you come out of the storm, you won't be the same person who walked in.' In Padmanabhan's case, it was literal. In the agency, it was one of my favourite tales. I never met Padmanabhan, again, though I do remember this incident with fondness, and it makes me smile, as I'm doing right now.

The Price Paid For Revenue Growth

Lata Subramanian

One of the CBI (Central Bureau of Investigation) officers in the room leaned over to pat my hand and said, 'Madam, please don't worry. We know you had nothing to do with this. But we have to ask the questions.'

His colleague and fellow CBI officer nodded his head in agreement.

I doubt their reassurances worked on me at that point in time because I was pretty much frozen in terror.

How did I, an ordinary middle-class girl, land up being questioned by the CBI at all? It just didn't happen to honest, hardworking people. At least that's what I grew up believing.

There I was in one of the cabins at the advertising agency, Lintas[1], surrounded by files and 2 CBI officers.

It all began a few months prior when I received a phone call from an ex-client whose account I had worked on in my previous agency, Trikaya[2]. The call was to say that her current employer wanted to know if Lintas would help him release an advertisement. The employer in question was Harshad Mehta[3] or Harshad Bhai[4], as he was more popularly addressed.

I had never heard of Harshad Mehta or his company because, at that time, I had little idea of the doings in the stock market. On the salary I was earning then, I was hardly able to save a couple of hundred bucks let alone

____

[1]Lintas, over the years, has merged several times with other advertising agencies within the IPG advertising network. The agency is now known as Mullen Lowe Lintas Group.

[2]Trikaya was later acquired by the global agency, Grey. Over time, the agency came to be known as Grey Advertising.

[3]Harshad M. Mehta was an Indian stockbroker who was dubbed the Big Bull in India. He was later the prime accused in one of India's biggest stock scams. He died in 2002 when he was in judicial custody in Thane prison near Mumbai.

[4]*Bhai*, meaning brother in several Indian languages, is used as a respectful suffix to first names in most parts of India; particularly so in the Gujarati community. In recent decades, the term *bhai* has also served as a suffix to the names of gangsters, after the usage was popularized by Bollywood movies.

invest in shares. That said, I was thrilled when I received the call from my ex-client because I imagined I was living out the truth of what David Ogilvy[5] had said in his famous, timeless in relevance, book Ogilvy On Advertising - clients who respected and trusted you come back to you with more business! I should mention that I am unsure if the principle I am talking about here was from the book mentioned above or his earlier publication, Confessions of an Advertising Man[6].

Anyway, I was highly excited at the prospect of bringing in new business for the agency. More so, because I was only an Account Supervisor at that time, and I knew that bagging an account would go down well with the agency management and do wonders for my career.

In that frame of mind, I went and met Harshad Mehta with stars in my eyes. Since I was still fairly junior, the head of the Strategic Business Unit (SBU) I was working in accompanied me.

The result of that meeting was a newspaper advertisement that triggered off a maelstrom in India and in my life.

---

[5]David Ogilvy was the founder of Ogilvy & Mather (now just Ogilvy) and is widely known as the Father of Advertising. Originally published in 1983, Ogilvy on Advertising is a book that is timeless in its relevance

[6]*Confessions of an Advertising Man* was published in 1963 by David Ogilvy. The book is still used to teach young advertising professionals some classic principles of the profession.

Designed to issue a disclaimer that Harshad Mehta, the Big Bull of India's stock market, was manipulating Apollo Tyres' shares, the half-page newspaper ad ran with a screaming headline that read 'Harshad Mehta is a Liar.[7]'

In my career, no other advertisement I worked on became the talk of the town as this one did. It literally made newspaper readers that morning sit up and take notice. Stories of how people had been overheard discussing the ad in commuter trains, buses and on the street poured into the agency that day.

There was huge excitement in the agency that an ad it had created had made such an impact. But it was nothing compared to Harshad bhai's reaction. He was over the moon. I guess the ad confirmed to him that stock market investors were ready to follow him in creating what he envisioned as the biggest bull run India would ever witness. Who knows, but in all likelihood, he had begun to see himself as the Warren Buffett of India.

The other fall-out of the ad was that Harshad Mehta now wanted to harness the power of advertising to bring about a paradigm shift in India's thinking about the role of the stock market in realising the country's economic potential. Of course, needless to say, the Big Bull saw his company, GrowMore, as playing a pivotal role in making that happen!

---

[7]The "Harshad Mehta is a Liar" ad was attributed as one of the causes that triggered the downfall of India's Big Bull.

He shared his vision with the agency and asked for a corporate communications campaign to help achieve it.

I saw it as a highly exciting brief from a client. Here was an opportunity to create a campaign that could fire up a whole nation.

The question before me was simply how to come up with a brief to the creative team, which would result in such an impactful campaign.

The answer just fell into place one day when my mind connected a few dots. The dots were there in the reams of reading I had undertaken to understand the role of stock markets in buoyant economies.

Post the liberalisation of the Indian economy in 1991; the country was abuzz with excitement. India had been unshackled. It was akin to second independence.

India had great potential. It had a market of some 1 billion people. Imagine what would happen if all that energy was to be harnessed?

To achieve that potential, however, attitudes had to change, and the nation united to achieve its economic goals.

A company that ran ads to that effect would be seen as a thought leader and visionary.

Those were the dots. The brief I issued to creative used phrases such as:

- India needs to undertake an economic war much like Japan did at one time.

- India needs to forget about its religious differences and unite in a new religion – the religion of economics.

- A nation with a population of 1 billion could be the biggest Bull Run in the world history of the stock market.

- India needs a second independence movement.

The outcome of that brief was a print campaign with headlines that went:

'India needs a new religion'.

'India should go to war'.

I don't remember the 3rd ad, but I think it had something to do with the second independence movement.

Harshad bhai loved the campaign. I didn't even have to try selling the work. It just sold itself. Post that and other similar experiences, I am known to frequently say, 'Good work sells itself.'

I knew I had a blockbuster of a campaign in the bag. Flushed with that excitement, I presented the work internally to Alyque Padamsee[8] and Prem Mehta[9]. They

---

[8]Alyque Padamsee is a well-known figure in Indian advertising and theatre circles. Internationally, and beyond advertising and theatre circles, he is perhaps better known for his role as Jinnah in Richard Attenborough's film *Gandhi*.

[9]Prem Mehta later took on the mantle of CEO Lintas when Alyque

were delighted when they saw the work and called in scores of people in the agency to see it. Alyque even sent the campaign to the Prime Minister's office.

I was stunned by the impact of the work and over the moon.

Life has this way of bringing you quickly down to earth though. I know it did so in this case because as it turned out, the campaign never saw the light of day.

In November 1992, Harshad Mehta was arrested on multiple counts of fraud. As we learnt, the Big Bull was exploiting a loophole in the Indian banking system to finance his stock market investments and manipulations.

It was post his arrest that the CBI landed up at the Lintas office, demanding that the agency give them access to all the files on the account and the people handling Harshad Mehta's business.

That's how I ended up being interrogated by the CBI. They specifically asked for me because my signature had been logged in the entry register at the Finance Ministry in Delhi.

Why? It may sound incredible, but I had accompanied Harshad Mehta to Delhi to operate a slide projector while he was making a presentation to the Finance Secretary on his vision for the stock market.

Padamsee retired in 1993 or thereabouts. Prem has since retired from Lintas and is currently Chairman, Northpoint Centre of Learning; a Management Development institution he conceived and established in Lonavala near Mumbai.

I swear to God that was my only role. I shouldn't have gone, but Harshad Mehta did not know how to operate a 35mm slide projector and its remote. He demanded that the agency produce his slides and send someone to help him in Delhi. Of course, the agency readily agreed for a client it deemed important.

Honestly, I didn't mind either. I was, in fact, excited at the prospect of witnessing the presentation.

Months later, facing two CBI officers, I bitterly regretted having accompanied the Big Bull to Delhi. Not just that. I wished the agency had turned away his business altogether.

A word here on the CBI officers would be in order. As I have already mentioned, both officers went out of their way to be kind to me. But here's the thing. As memory serves, they interrogated me for some 8 hours. The day it happened I was too frozen with terror to absorb what was happening. But later when I looked back, my respect for the CBI went up. They were not the monsters they are often made out to be. And boy, were they skilled in the art of interrogation. They kept asking questions over and over till they drew out every single memory I never even knew I had retained in the recesses of my brain. Slowly and surely, the CBI officers drew out those memories of my visit to the Finance Ministry in Delhi. It was as if they possessed an invisible pensieve[10] in their arsenal.

---

[10]Pensieve is a memory enhancer made famous by the Harry Potter novels

I learnt something that day. I sure did. But the biggest learning from working on the Harshad Mehta account was simply this. It's true that everything that glitters is not gold. One has to look beyond the cover to examine the contents before striking a deal. If there is even a whiff that all is not kosher, I would say it's better to turn away business and forego revenue growth.

It is a lesson I have never forgotten, influencing the way I evaluated business opportunities forever thereafter.

I will say one thing though. Somewhere I still hold the dream of that unreleased campaign running to good effect. Think about it. The messages there are more relevant than ever for India and its people.

Why I Hate Textbooks

Sumit Roy

I want to tear up every college textbook that I see. This story is about why.

I am surprised that I agreed to write for Sanjeev's book. I hope it never becomes a textbook. Because I hate textbooks.

If you are reading this book to get better marks at school or college, please tear this chapter out.

Actually, I guess it is education by rote that I hate.

For 39 years of my life, I thought that's how education was meant to be. You sit in a class and you memorise the books that your teacher tells you to. You'd better do that; otherwise you won't get the marks you need to compete with the rest of the class.

Your career will be ruined.

Balderdash.

I hate that system of education. Makes us birdbrained parrots.

Which is why I felt such an epiphany when I saw Robin Williams play the character, John Keating, in Dead Poets' Society.

Here was a teacher who got his students to tear up a textbook that made poetry a mathematical model. He got students to stand up on their benches so that they could experience things differently. He exhorted his students: 'make your lives extraordinary. Carpe Diem. Seize the day.'

If you haven't seen Dead Poets Society consider yourself uneducated. You haven't yet learnt how to reach your potential.

Stop reading this book and download the movie now.

After a magical run in advertising through the 70s and the 80s, in 1991, I was ready to start a school of advertising. I saw an opportunity in the fact that advertising agencies liked to hire people with at least one year's work experience.

What I was not sure about was the shape that the school of advertising and brand-building communication should take.

Then I saw Dead Poets Society.

It all started making sense. The best way to learn is to learn by doing. Advertising was not a science. It was poetry. Just that it was poetry with a purpose.

After seeing Dead Poets Society, I was ready to brief Adi Pocha for the entrance brochure to the school I wanted to start.

Adi Pocha and I left Lintas at the same time. Not that we wanted to leave together. Just that we were both ready to start our own thing. He started ScriptShop which evolved to become Squirkle. I started Univads, which evolved to become Univbrands.

But we had a symbiotic relationship. I think the Univads brochure was one of the first writing assignments that Adi got as ScriptShop.

I told Adi about my Dead Poets Society epiphany. I added my twist on it. The students in my school would learn by earning. The only marks they would get would be a cheque at the end of the month. Once they started earning more than they would get if they joined an agency, then I would place them, within one year of 'work experience', which is all that this advertising school offered. No classes. No lectures.

For the cost of writing the copy for the entrance brochure to Univads, a learn-by-earning school of advertising and brand-building communication, Adi Pocha gave me a branding idea that has lasted me, now, for more than 25 years. It has evolved, but it is still going strong.

The headline of the brochure read: The Theoretical Bicyclist.

It went on to argue that, just like it was impossible to ride a bicycle by reading a manual, it was impossible to learn advertising without doing advertising.

Univads would also not have happened if Ronnie Screwvala had not shown me how to start a company with just Rs. 1000.

Ronnie was a theatre friend. We had produced rock concerts together, as far back as 1974. I explained the idea of a learn-by-earning school of advertising to Ronnie. Either I was very good at explaining the idea, or Ronnie was good at spotting the potential. Somehow, I think it was the latter.

Ronnie made me an offer I could not refuse. I could use the Unilazer offices to run my 'learn-by-earning school' as long as I became a director on the board of his group of companies. The Uni in the Univads and later Univbrands is really a nod to Ronnie and what was then the Unilazer Group.

On the strength of the brochure, and the fact that students did not have to pay for the course – instead, they earned – word of mouth spread quickly. I soon had the first batch of Univads students.

Revenues came from the advertising that the students created for entrepreneurs and retail outlets who paid 5 to10% of their sales, after they got the sales. The 'clients' did not have to pay for the advertising. There was never a shortage of clients.

Revenues also came from advertising agencies that passed on work that they found unglamorous: brochures, audio-visuals, sales conference material, quick and dirty market research.

Grunt work that I knew the students would have to learn to do and which were not usually required by the 'retail clients' that were our bread and butter.

The students learnt to be entrepreneurs and risked their time. I showed them how to collect money from the revenues they generated before settling their expenses. Since media gave 45 days credit and suppliers could be negotiated to give 60 days credit, without a single class on business management, they learnt how to do business.

I never had to pass judgement on copy or art. I left it to the students to risk their ideas. All I insisted on was that the proofing and the detailing won them a reputation for being perfectionists.

If the ideas worked, they got paid. If the ideas didn't, they learnt. None of the ideas could stray from a document I made them write on each brand they handled.

The document had to be written in English. Jargon was not allowed.

1. What business is the brand really in? (Is this based on an emotional need?)

2. Therefore, at whom is the brand aimed?

3. If the brand were a person, what three adjectives should be used?

4. What's the continuing idea for the brand that the consumer will want to champion?

They had no idea that they were writing, by just using their common sense and astute observations, what most people in the profession struggle to write, after several years of experience, while using models, charts and reams of analysis.

The secret was that I encouraged them to leave the comfort of their desks in their search for answers.

What they learnt to do, very quickly, was to talk to consumers and get to understand them. If there was a classroom that they had, it was the streets of Mumbai.

When it came to the actual production of the work, the students could hire their own faculty. Every Freelancer – Writers, Art Directors, Photographers, Film Directors, Editing Studio, Print Production House – was effectively 'faculty'. My job was to tell the students who would be the best resource to learn, and earn, from.

My deal with the 'faculty' was that they would get 75% of their normal fees. And since the Univads students would keep 25% of that fee, they should get the students to do most of the work.

This arrangement seemed good for the Freelancers. They got assignments that they would never have got. And they got a team of enthusiastic learners to do the work, under their guidance. It was certainly good for the students. They earned on the job.

I learnt too. Along with the students, I got very good at helping people answer the common sense questions that help build brands that consumers want to champion.

I also discovered that there were more ways to grow brands than just advertising. The revenues were often coming from ideas that went beyond the area of paid media. It was the mid 1990s and the Univads students had already understood the power of earned media and owned media. After all, it was their money.

Soon, Univads was ready to evolve into becoming Univbrands. And the internet had a very strong role to play in that evolution.

Because of the money generating ideas that the Univads students were coming up with, often in the area of product, pricing, placement and self-financing promotions, Univads was ready to become Univbrands.

By that time Ronnie Screwvala had also got his solution of how to have enough money to have UTV House, the agreed benchmark to know that UTV was now a stable brand.

One presentation to Rupert Murdoch was enough. That done, I handed Ronnie the Rs. 1000 with which he helped me start this amazing journey and rechristened Univads to become Univbrands. Univbrands was now mine.

Then, quite by accident, I discovered that the common sense brand building questions I was getting the Univads students to answer in plain English, allowed me to help home-based and small entrepreneurs across the world make their businesses sustainable brands.

The Univads model had a huge flaw. I was the bottleneck. Everything had to pass my eagle eye. While Freelancers were aplenty, I could not get anyone else to give up their jobs and do what I was doing.

Make sure that the work was always 'on brand'. Orchestrate print with radio, packaging with pricing, audio-visual with press release, photography with mailing lists, typeface with sound-track.

For the four years that I ran Univads, I realised that I had completely neglected my family while I took to parenting just four to eight students at a time.

Then came the Internet. And the Candlelady incident.

'Candlelady' is the handle that I still know her as. When I met her online, she had recently divorced and was struggling to earn $5000 a month. She lived in Connecticut and was making candles at home and was trying to sell them to her friends.

I met her in the online chat room of www.talkcity. com called #bizcenter where home-based entrepreneurs, across the USA, would gather. Fascinated by the sharing economy of the net, I used to help these entrepreneurs answer the four common sense brand-building questions that I was now using for the Univbrands students.

During one online chat show, with a chat room full of other home-based entrepreneurs, I asked Candlelady, 'What business are you really in?'

'Candles,' said Candlelady. The others in the room agreed.

'No,' I said, having learnt well from my Univads/ Univbrands students. 'You are in the Romance business'.

To Candlelady's credit, she understood immediately.

While the chat show continued online, she had opened a private chat box and messaged me: 'How much will you charge to coach me how to make my business a romance brand?' Or words to that effect.

I was caught off-guard. I hadn't worked out what I should charge a divorcee in Connecticut who wanted to know how to ride the brand building motorcycle.

So far I had not been charging the students that I taught to ride the brand building motorcycle. They paid me from their earnings. But companies who wanted me to run on-the-job coaching programs for their Management Trainees were paying me a fee.

Multi-tasking away with the several questions that the 'romance' comment had generated in the chat room, I converted what Coca-Cola India was then paying me each month to run weekly learn-by-doing workshops for their Management Trainees: '$1500,' I typed, in the private chat box with Candlelady.

There was a long pause at the other end.

I panicked as I thought that I had quoted too high. I started having qualms about the poor divorcee in Connecticut who didn't have a job. So I invented, there and then, a pricing policy that has held me in good stead to this day.

The following two texts happened simultaneously.

'50% of the fees upfront. The balance when you get to your revenue target,' I texted.

'Is that all?' she had texted.

Clearly, we had sent out our messages together.

That's when I realised that $1500 was nothing to someone in the US of A to learn how to make her business into a brand.

Especially since Diane Garrod, who was in charge of the TalkCity chat rooms, had profiled me as someone who conducts training sessions for Coca-Cola, Kellogg's, Unilever, McKinsey & Co ... which was true. Just that it was in India.

Candlelady asked: 'When can we start?'

'How will you pay me?' I responded.

'Send me your account details, and I will wire you the money,' texted Candlelady. And as simple as that, Candlelady had taught me how to take my coaching business online.

The next day, I found the equivalent of $750 in my bank.

I knew I had to show her how to get to $5000 a month. Three months later, using the very techniques that I had learnt from my learn-by-earning students in Mumbai, I had shown Candlelady how to reach her desired income of $5000 a month.

Carpe Diem, Robin Williams playing John Keating had said. Seize the day.

So that day, when Candlelady gave me the opportunity to move my learn-by-earning school of brand-building online, I did. Now my income comes from places as far away as Santiago and Sydney.

The best way to learn is to learn by earning. Just find someone to show you the gears.

Self Notes:
Reflect. Absorb. Move On

Let's do an exercise. Here is the good news. A well-known publisher wants to publish your autobiography. The only condition is that it cannot have more than FIVE CHAPTERS. So he has asked you to share the five most important episodes of your life. He wants you to REFLECT why they are most important and why did you chose them. Then write down what were your learning's from these life-episodes? Have you ABSORBED the learning? And have you now MOVED ON?

____

____

____

____

____

____

Arvind Passy

Arvind Passey began his professional life marching up and down the drill square of the Indian Military Academy as a gentleman cadet and ended his job-era playing hide-&-seek with media teams as the Head of Corporate Communications.

A few of the 1800+ poems written by him are published in journals in India & UK but the rest still in notebooks, loose sheets, penned on napkins, and in computer files. He has had short-stories published in anthologies and articles in The Education Post, HT, TOI, The Huffington Post, Business Insider, & MarketingBuzzar and various other publications. He dreams of travelling to every country in the world... and of finally completing his first novel. On the social media, he is /Arvind Passey everywhere. Blog: http://passey.info

Farzana Suri

After bidding goodbye to a successful career in advertising, creating brands, Farzana Suri followed the nudge of the universe. She established Farzana Suri Victory Coach, and she coaches people through the twisting curves of life's journey using a spectrum of tools including NLP, Numerology and Graphology. As a Victory Coach, she has empowered over 5000 people to see the Brand in themselves and, to be what they are born to be – Victors!

She specialises in helping individuals and groups to achieve personal and professional goals through the power of coaching and make the mental shifts required to sustain change. She is a Life Coach, Keynote Speaker and Corporate Trainer. She integrates therapies to get to the heart of the problem. Hailing from the land of nawabs, she is a foodie, poet, cat lover, humanist and avid traveller.

Her mantra in life is, 'I want to inspire people. I want people to look at me and say, 'Because of YOU, I didn't give up.'

Harrish M Bhatia

Mr. Harrish M Bhatia is the Chief Executive Officer of MY FM, the Radio Business of DB Corp Ltd. and the driving force behind the station's record-breaking performance in the short span of its existence. Starting in 2007, he led the MY FM brand through successful launches of all stations, to operational break-even in just three years and turning PAT positive within five years of operation. As an agile, versatile and multi-tasking individual, he has been spearheading innovations within the brand and the business operations to maintain the dynamic performance of MY FM. Under his visionary leadership, MY FM has been delivering outstanding performance quarter after quarter, making it a dominant player in the national radio space. During his tenure at MY FM, Mr. Bhatia's efforts have been recognised through several awards which have been bestowed on the radio station as well as on him individually.

He is an old hand at Bhaskar and has to his credit the launch of Divya Bhaskar (newspaper) in Gujarat in 2003 and Dainik Bhaskar in Jaipur. Before joining Bhaskar, he had served as the Product Head at the Korean Multinational LG Electronics in India He has extensive experience in setting up new projects and turning around operations.

Kyati

Khyati is a marketing professional with more than 13 years of diverse exposure and rich experience in Advertising, Brand Management, Fragrance and Media Marketing.

She has served as India marketing manager for International Flavours and Fragrance, has been in a brand management role with ICICI Prudential and client servicing profile with the advertising agencies like Grey World Wide, Ogilvy & Mather and Triton Communications.

Currently, she is working with Dainik Bhaskar as General Manager.

Besides expressing her creativity in professional life, she loves letting loose her paintbrush and pen, an avid reader and loves to learn new languages.

Solo traveller, she thrives on challenges, loves exploring less travelled destinations and soon going to aggregate her solo travel expedition into blogs.

Lata Subramanian

An Economics graduate, Lata has over 35 years of work experience across a range of service-related industries such as Advertising, Civil Aviation, Hospitality, Marketing and Publishing.

She is a voracious reader and loves to write. Her love for writing led her to accept the post of Managing Editor, The Smart Manager; a position she held between 2008 and 2010 when she was in Publishing. She is now a hobbyist writer and blogger, publishing blogs regularly on www.latawonders.com

Lata has just hung up her boots, retiring from corporate life to blog and maybe write a book or two or take up a few consultancy assignments. The last position Lata held in the corporate world was CMO, Sterling Holiday Resorts (India) Limited - a leading Leisure Hospitality and Vacation Ownership company in India.

Lata's favourite description of herself is that she is a student of life and herself. That lifelong interest has led to her first book A Dance with the Corporate Ton: Reflections of a Worker Ant.

The book is available on Amazon Kindle.

Neeraj Basur

Neeraj Basur is a finance professional with over 25 years multi-sector experience. His forte is strategic financial management and grooming high performing finance teams. In the past, he has been a part of senior management teams at Max Bupa, Max India and HCL Technologies. His experience cuts across Corporate and Operating Finance roles. In the past, he has been associated with start-up business ventures as well. He specialises in the financial, strategic and structural transformation of organisations to enhance shareholder value.

He is currently associated as the Chief Financial Officer of Blue Star.

Neeraj is fond of travelling and loves spending time close to nature. He loves playing keyboard and bongo during his free time. He writes blogs and chronicles on topics around functional and leadership excellence.

Prabhakar Mundkur

Prabhakar Mundkur is an ad veteran and has spent over 38 years in advertising. Besides working in India, he has also worked across the African Continent based in Nairobi and Johannesburg and in Asia when he was based in Shanghai. He has been in senior management and CEO positions for the last 20 years with advertising networks like JWT, Havas, Y & R and Hakuhodo.

He currently consults with a number of companies. He is on the Advisory Board of AKG Technologies and Sol's Arc and Chief Mentor with HGS Interactive a part of the Hinduja Group.

In his spare time, he is listening to or playing music. He was an HMV and Polydor recording artist in his teens and continues to play jazz guitar and do the occasional gig with his friends because he thinks it is fun. He has recently become a compulsive blogger.

Raja Mitra

 Raja, a Mechanical Engineering graduate from Jadavpur University, Kolkata, Raja completed his PGDM in Marketing & Finance from I.I.M.-Bangalore(1993-95). He has got more than 20 years of senior Management experience across a wide gamut of domains, viz. Engineering, B2B, dotcom, media, etc.

He has also been an entrepreneur in his life. An International Coach Federation Certified Life Coach with a niche in Career transition, Raja, has been an aggressive and professional with a very high level of integrity. An inspirational leader, he has achieved leadership success in most assignments that he has handled in his career.

Raman Kalia

Raman Kalia is a brand strategist and an innovation consultant with 20 years of experience in diverse industries. He has been associated with organisations like TATA, UB Group, Air Deccan, BIAL, FCB and DDB Mudra.

During his stint with Bangalore Airport, he conceptualised, designed and introduced a tourism concept 'Kaapi Trail' in collaboration with Tourism Department (GoK), Coffee Board of India. He was also a member of KTVG (Karnataka Tourism Vision Group), an initiative of Ministry of Tourism, Government of Karnataka for developing and promoting the state tourism ecosystem.

Raman is a co-founder of Think Simplr (thinksimplr. com), a brand and culture transformation agency. He is an author of two books and his latest book 'Brand Cliches: Conventional Thinking to Build Extraordinary Brands' is available in the market.

Sanhita Baruah

Sanhita Baruah, 25, born and brought-up in Guwahati, Assam, and an MBA from MDI, Gurgaon. She has been blogging since January 2012 and has also contributed short stories and poems for National and International anthologies including Curtain Call, A World Rediscovered, Kaleidoscope, Minds @ Work 2, etc. Her articles find a place in journals and magazines including North East Today, Good Times of the North-East, Fried Eye, Word Splash, Springtide, etc.

She has been writing poems since the age of 11, and a collection of some of her best poems has been published as an e-book titled 'The Farewell.' As she attempts to leave an emotional imprint on the readers with each of her work, she believes people can bring about a change with what they write and what they read.

She blogs at http://sanhitabaruah9.blogspot.in/

Sanjeev Kotnala

Sanjeev is an Engineer with PGDBM from IIM Ahmedabad. He is a complete optimist and a romantic at heart. He has over 28 years of experience in Marketing and Brand Management. He invested his first 17 years of professional life in advertising with reputed leading agencies Mudra, HTA (JWT) and Lintas.

After his last corporate roles as Vice President National Marketing with Dainik Bhaskar Group, he started INTRADIA WORLD as an Independent Brand and Marketing advisor, Trainer, facilitator and accredited coach.

His conducts unique specialised interactive workshops IdeaHARVEST- co-creating and Harvesting ideas, Liberate process of inclusive decision, InNoWait- for Innovating you need not wait and BRAND-i- treating yourself as a brand.

Sanjeev is a regular blogger at www.sanjeevkotnala. com. He writes a weekly column KOTMARTIAL on advertising media and marketing at www.mxmindia.com.

He is a voracious reader, and founder of '50 books challenge India', a painter, storyteller and doodler. Sanjeev has won many awards and was listed as top 500 people in media and advertising in India.

Sumit Roy

He learnt how to build brands in the 14 years that he spent with Ogilvy & Mather, and he learnt how to grow people who grow brands in the 4 years he spent with Lintas.

He now runs the world's smallest online learn-by-earning university of brand building from Kolkata, www.univbrands.com. It is the world's smallest because it has only one employee. Him. But the 'students' are many, spread across USA, Canada, Chile, UK, France, Spain, Italy, Russia, South Africa, Bahrain, UAE, Mauritius, Sri Lanka, Nepal, Bangladesh, Malaysia, Singapore, Australia and of course, India.

Apart from coaching online, he runs workshops on Integrated Brand Building, Idea Management and Presentation Skills, where there are no lectures, nor any theoretical sessions. The workshop participants, ranging from management trainees to CEOs, learn by doing.

Tanya Kotnala

'Illustrations, surface texturing and crafts' fashion design presently occupy Tanya Kotnala but finding usual things unite to form something unusual, surreal is what drives her aesthetics. Her illustration and crafts fashion page 'Bhuli' is an attempt to present contemporary | traditional arts and crafts of India in the most honest and modern fashion.

Drawing for this book was one of the most interesting projects I've illustrated so far, it was inspiring to read and experience real-life stories shared by the top management professionals of India.

Vikas Mehta

Having worked as a marketing communication professional in India, Far East, Middle East and North Africa with agencies like Lowe, JWT and Havas, Vikas is currently learning the ropes of a small town Bhartiya, out of Dehradun. The transition from being a CEO, Regional Brand Head and Strategic Planning Head to understanding what makes the small Indian city tick, has turned Vikas into a student once again. And interacting with students at various business and communication institutes as Guest Faculty has been equally exhilarating as having worked on brands like Lifebuoy, Horlicks, Kitply, Hero, Philips, Surf, Pepsodent, Sony, Emirates SkyCargo, J&J, HSBC, Nissan, Oman Air amongst others.

His experiences amongst different cultures, consumers and categories make for a fascinating read, rich in situations and anecdotes. Visit him at http://www.admaadmusings.com

Also By
Sanjeev Kotnala

The lives of five residents of the sleepy little town of Lansdowne in Uttarakhand is loosely connected. They have all been at the receiving end of independent unexplained experiences. Their past is intertwined with their present and maybe the future, in case it exists.

They can only succeed collectively by joining forces. However, success is one of the many possibilities. They don't know the unseen. They have no idea what the *Cinemera of Lansdowne* is. They must explore the only direction they have.

Will they come together to take advantage of a once in a lifetime alignment of celestial bodies? Time like always is limited. Will they be able to connect all the dots and find the key? Will they succeed in breaking the cycle?

INR 185. Available At Amazon, Flipkart AND Notion Press